QUICKBOOKS® ONLINE
for
NONPROFITS & CHURCHES

A STEP-BY-STEP GUIDE

Second Edition

Lisa London, CPA

Deep River Press, Inc.

Morehead City, North Carolina

QuickBooks Online for Nonprofits & Churches -A Step-By Step Guide

ISBN 978-1-945561-19-1

Library of Congress Control Number: 2024902201

Published by Deep River Press, Inc. March 2024

Edited by Linda Peterson

Books by Lisa London

- *The Accountant Beside You series*
- *BANISH Your Bookkeeping Nightmares*
- *QuickBooks® for Nonprofit s & Churches-The Step-by-Step Guide to the Pro, Premier, and Nonprofit Versions*
- *Nonprofit Accounting for Volunteers, Treasurers, and Bookkeepers*
- *Church Accounting—The How-To Guide for Small & Growing Churches*
- *QuickBooks® for Churches and Other Religious Organizations*
- *QuickBooks® para Iglesias y Otras Organizaciones Religiosas*

Historical Fiction

- *Darker the Night*

TABLE OF CONTENTS

1

QUICKBOOKS ONLINE & NONPROFITS

I f you are dreading the thought of setting up or taking over the bookkeeping for a small nonprofit or house of worship, I am here to make it manageable. My motto is *Keep it simple.* I am going to walk you through the nonprofit specific terminology you need to know, teach you what the QuickBooks limitations are for nonprofit organizations and provide work arounds, and help you design internal accounting controls. Then, you'll learn how to set up your organization's accounting system, pay bills, and receive money through the system. Month and year-end reporting and review will be covered, and finally, you'll learn some unusual and infrequent items that you need to consider.

My approach is designed to get you quickly and easily up and running on the process's nonprofits use often and find the most important. This book is not meant to be read once and forgotten. Keep it close to the computer, use what you need, and check my website, www.accountantbesideyou.com, for more tips, videos, discussions, and updates. Remember, as The Accountant Beside You, I am with you all the way. Let's get started.

A. WILL QUICKBOOKS ONLINE WORK FOR MY ORGANIZATION?

The QuickBooks programs are not designed for nonprofits but can work up to a point that is acceptable for most organizations. This book is designed to show you how to make it work for your nonprofit needs.

 Note: For simplicity sake, all nonprofit organizations, churches, associations, and clubs will be referred to as organizations, and QuickBooks® will be QuickBooks or QuickBooks Online (QBO).

QuickBooks is available in a desktop subscription version for PCs and an online version. Each is similar, but independent programs. This book will cover only the online version.

If you are running QuickBooks desktop, I recommend reading *QuickBooks for Nonprofits & Churches-A Step-By-Step Guide to the Pro, Premier, and Nonprofit Versions.*

There are four basic QuickBooks Online (QBO) subscription levels: **Simple Start, Essentials, +New,** and **Advanced**. Payroll and merchant services can be added to any of the subscriptions. Because you can only use the **Class** feature (to be discussed in a later chapter) in the **+New** and **Advanced** offerings, I do not recommend a nonprofit use either the **Simple Start** or the **Essentials** options. Your data is automatically backed up, and accountant users can be invited at no added charge. Qualified nonprofits and churches may be able to buy a one-year subscription from Techsoup.org for $75.00. Techsoup is a nonprofit dedicated to matching other nonprofits with technology solutions.

They receive donations from technology companies and give them to qualifying nonprofits for a small handling fee. It is a wonderful resource, and I highly recommend that you check out their website, www.techsoup.org, for all your technological needs. (Please note, I have no affiliation with Techsoup. It is simply a valuable resource I want you to be aware of.)

To help you see the differences in the versions, here is a chart listing the features of each QBO subscription level.

QuickBooks Online Subscription Levels			
Features	Essentials	Plus	Advanced
Monthly cost	$60	$90	$200
Number of users	3	5	25
Number of built in reports	40+	65+	65+
Track income and expenses	√	√	√
Create and send invoices	√	√	√
Print checks and record transactions	√	√	√
Download bank and credit card transactions	√	√	√
Backup data automatically	√	√	√
Import data from Excel and QuickBooks Desktop	√	√	√

Invite up to two accountant users to access your data	√	√	√
Access data from a tablet or smartphone	√	√	√
Control what users can access	√	√	√
Manage, schedule, and pay bills	√	√	√
Create and send purchase orders		√	√
Prepare and print 1099s		√	√
Create budgets ***		√	√
Use class tracking ***		Up to 40	unlimited
Use location tracking***		Up to 40	unlimited
Project tracking		√	√
Track inventory		√	√

If you have employees, QuickBooks offers payroll services that can be added to any of the QBO accounting service levels. I will explain each of the options and how to enter the data in Chapter 10.

*Class tracking and the ability to create budgets are very important for nonprofits and churches, therefore the only levels of QBO I recommend is the **+New** and **Advanced** levesl. QuickBooks support may tell you the Simple Start or Essentials options will work, but they do not understand the complexities of nonprofit accounting.*

B. ADVANTAGES OF QBO

There are many reasons for an organization to move their accounting system to the cloud.

Flexibility and convenience are QBO's biggest advantages. Your organization's accounting records can be accessed from any internet-connected PC or mobile device. The executive director or pastor can review reports even if they are not in the office. The volunteer treasurer can work from home. You aren't tied to working only in the office. A mobile app is available for your phone to see financial data on the go and there are many third-party applications to help with specific fun.

Multiple users at separate locations can use the program or view reports simultaneously. The treasurer can be online reviewing the previous month's financial statements while the bookkeeper is inputting this week's donations. If the members of your board of directors live in separate cities, each can review the reports online while on a joint conference call or Skype session. This is a contrast from the software for desktop versions which is found on a single computer and can usually only be accessed from that location, though a cloud hosting or sharing service is sometimes used at an added monthly cost.

There is no need to backup data because your work is automatically saved by QBO. The desktop version must be backed up and the files kept in a secure location. If your computer crashes or you are moving the accounting system to a different unit, you can simply log into your QBO account instead of having to restore the data manually.

Bank data is fed automatically, always giving you an up-to-date view of your cash situations. The desktop version will allow you to import your bank data, but it will not be automatic.

Your professional accountant can be given access to the system, which can save time and effort for both the organization's staff and the accountant. Your accountant can use QBO's accountants' tools to add to the value of the services offered. In the desktop version, you must set up a special Accountant's File to send for review, determine a date so you and the accountant are changing data in the same accounting period, and then restore the Accountant's File.

With a QBO subscription, there is no need to install updates to receive new features. QuickBooks Online is always current.

C. FUND ACCOUNTING

Not-for-profit organizations do not work the same way as for-profit organizations; nor do they account for revenues and expenses the same way. Historically, the accounting for nonprofit organizations was called Fund Accounting because each designated "pot of money" was accounted for in a different fund. Currently, organizations are using a "net asset" model based on what restrictions were placed on the donations when they were received.

The Financial Accounting Standards Board (FASB) has issued new accounting standards for nonprofits. These are primarily reporting changes. If you are large enough to require financial statements presented with Generally Accepted Accounting Principles (GAAP), you will need to work with a CPA to see how these changes affect you. For the purposes of this book, I am going to assume you need an accounting system that will generate financial reports to help manage your organization and be a good steward of the donors' gifts, but I will not be addressing the accounting standards.

An organization may receive donations from many different areas: membership dues, pledges or tithes, general support of the organization, an outreach program, a capital campaign, or maybe an endowment. Some of the money given, like the dues, is considered "without donor restriction." It is assumed the organization will use this money as needed, and the donor has not requested any limitations on the use of the funds.

Other times, money will be received for a specific purpose—an outreach program or a capital campaign, or for a specific time—say next year's dues. Then the money is considered "with donor restrictions". This means it can only be used for the purpose or period the donor has specified. When the restriction is met, i.e., the building is built or a new year has begun, then it becomes an asset "without donor restrictions".

In accounting jargon, nonprofit organizations are required to keep their accounting records using a modified form of fund accounting. **A fund is defined as a discrete accounting entity with its own set of accounts that must balance the cash and other assets against the liabilities and reserves of the organization**. That is a wordy way of saying each significant donation (funds given for specific purposes) should be tracked separately. But as most organizations don't keep separate bank accounts for each fund, you will be using a bit easier system called net assets to track the funds.

For reporting purposes, these funds can be combined by the restrictions placed on them and tracked by net assets. Net assets are the components of equity in the organization. It is what is left over after the liabilities (what is owed) are subtracted from the assets (what the organization owns). In the business world, this would be the accumulated profit or loss of the company and is called retained earnings. Net assets are currently divided into two categories:

1. Net Assets Without Donor Restrictions
2. Net Assets With Donor Restrictions.

Because it was designed for businesses which only have one retained earning account, QuickBooks cannot automatically record net earnings (donations less expenses) in each of the two types of net asset accounts. You will have to create the net asset equity accounts and use journal entries to move the balances from retained earnings.

D. REPORTING AND TERMINOLOGY DIFFERENCES

Financial reports for organizations also have different names than those for a business. The *Income Statement* or *Profit & Loss Statement* that tracks income and expenses for businesses is called **Statement of Activities** for nonprofits and churches. Assets, liabilities, and equity are tracked by companies in a *Balance Sheet*. A nonprofit uses a **Statement of Financial Position.** This is important as most versions of QuickBooks will list the reports using business terminology by default. For the purposes of this book, I'll refer to these reports as Profit & Loss Statement and Balance Sheet, to make it easier to find in the report menus. Here is a table showing the different terminology.

Description	Nonprofit Terminology	Church Terminology	QuickBooks Terminology
Your organization	Organization	Church, Parish, Synagogue, Temple	Company
People or organizations you receive money from	Donors, members, grantors, etc.	Parishioners, members, donors, etc.	Customers
People you pay money to	Vendors, suppliers, or people you reimburse	Vendors, suppliers, or people you reimburse	Vendors
Report to show money in versus money out (track income and expenses)	Statement of Activities	Statement of Activities	Income Statement or Profit & Loss Statement

Report to show assets (cash, property, etc.) against liabilities (amount owed) to track the accumulated net wealth	Statement of Financial Position	Statement of Financial Position	Balance Sheet
Accumulated net wealth/profit	Net Assets	Net Assets	Net Worth
Grants received that need to have the expenses tracked	Grants	Grants	Sub-Customers
Monies received for programs or that need to be tracked	Funds or programs	Funds or programs	Classes

While learning to use QBO, you may want to make a copy to have by your desk or to bookmark it for easy reference.

Although there are many limitations to the standard reporting that QuickBooks offers as it relates to organizations, Chapter 12 will go into detail on how to work around these limitations as you set up your reports.

By default, QuickBooks also refers to the people you receive money from as "Customers." Under company settings in QuickBooks Online, you may change the customer labels to one of the following: Clients, Donors, Guests, Members, Patients, or Tenants. The term selected will replace "Customer" wherever it's shown in QBO. I will explain how to change this label in Chapter 3.

Grants received will be tracked as "Sub-Customers," and designated monies and programs will be referred to as "Classes." Sub-customers and classes are ways the system tags information so reports can be run—pulling all the related data together. This terminology may sound strange, but it will become clearer as you go along.

E. THE CASE FOR INTERNAL ACCOUNTING CONTROLS

I know it's easy to think, "Why worry about accounting controls? Our employees and volunteers would never steal." With my experience as an auditor, I would beg to differ. As much as you would like that to be the case, it's not unusual for a donor or an employee to steal from a nonprofit. Do an internet search on "money stolen from nonprofits," and you will get over 3 million hits. Some of these were perpetrated by outsiders, but many of the news accounts mention administrators, bookkeepers, volunteers, and even pastors stealing.

Internal controls are not only in place to protect against fraud, but to keep errors from occurring and to make them easier to catch when they do. A good bookkeeper will require strong internal controls to keep themselves above suspicion. Additionally, you know that you wouldn't steal, but having controls in place gives you reassurance that the person who takes over after you will not either. The smaller the organization, the harder it is to have separate people in the required positions to support strong controls. But don't worry, this book will highlight options and ideas to put controls in place in even small nonprofits.

The most basic start for setting up internal controls begins at the governing body level (the board). A strong board with transparency, stewardship, and accountability sets the tone and is the first defense against fraud.

Because QuickBooks Online is accessible from any computer logged on to the internet, access controls need to be carefully thought out. Secure passwords are a must. Also, QBO allows for the setup of user profiles to create a segregation of duties. The master administrator of the company file can create limited user profiles that keep the user who handles recording donations from accessing bill paying and vice versa. I will explain user profiles in Chapter 3.

 *Your staff and volunteers need to understand that strong controls over the money keep them above suspicion!*

F. ADVICE FOR THE GOVERNING BODY OF THE ORGANIZATION

Members of the governing body have a fiduciary responsibility to the donors and employees. It is in their best interest to understand the internal controls of the organization. There are a few basic starting points for the board to consider.

1. Financial statements should be reviewed by the board on a regular basis (monthly or quarterly).

2. Annual budgets should be prepared, and variances reported on a regular basis.

3. There should be a designated treasurer who is NOT the bookkeeper.

4. A conflict-of-interest policy needs to be established. (This does not mean donors or board members can't do business with the organization. It simply limits the level of related party transactions and determines steps to make certain the most appropriate price is paid.)

5. An annual audit must be performed. If the organization cannot afford an outside auditor, appoint an audit committee composed of volunteers or board members not associated with the accounting part of the organization.

Within the chapters of this book, there will be recommendations for setting up the internal controls for each process of dealing with the finances. On my website, accountantbesideyou.com, I offer a companion handbook to help you in organizing your data with areas for you to detail your accounting controls procedures. If you have a CPA in your membership, you may wish to ask for more advice as well.

G. TIPS, HINTS, AND WHEN TO LET SOMEONE ELSE DO IT

Throughout this book, you will notice arrows and symbols with additional information.

 *These symbols are to alert you to tips and hints to make the work go easier or items that need special attention.*

There are additional resources at AccountantBesideYou.com. You can find free checklists, helpful videos, and supplemental items to buy that will help you save time.

Summary

In this chapter we covered the following:

- how to decide whether to use QBO or the desktop version,
- the basics of nonprofit accounting,
- how nonprofit accounting differs from for-profit accounting,
- the importance of internal accounting controls,
- and financial advice for the governing body of the organization.

Now let's look at how QuickBooks Online is used.

2

ACQUAINTING YOURSELF WITH QBO

A. LAYOUT OF THE PROGRAM

Before creating your company file or starting to enter data for your organization, I recommend you spend some time seeing how QBO is laid out and how to move around the program efficiently.

Fortunately, QBO has one sample "test drive" company called Craig's Design and Landscaping Services at https://qbo.intuit.com/redir/testdrive. This is a fully functioning practice company file with transactions already entered. I suggest you open the test company and follow along with the chapters to put what you are learning into practice. The menus will look a little different as the sample company screens aren't always updated, but they will allow you to get the basic feel.

You don't need an account or sign on to access the test drive, just a simple captcha code. Once accessed, you can add transactions, review reports, and explore functionality. This test drive is a place for you to explore and try out new things without the fear of breaking something or making a mistake. The practice company does not keep any of the changes you made. Please keep in mind, this test company is a for-profit company. Though the transactions and labels may be different than for nonprofits or churches, it will familiarize you with the system's functionality.

QBO is a database of tables and data fields. As you enter transactions, the system organizes your financial activity into financial results, so you can use what you've learned to make sound decisions for your organization. I know this can seem overwhelming, but I like CPA Eulica Kimber's advice to her clients—*always take your bookkeeping one transaction at a time*. This book will do just that, let's get started with the basics.

B. THE BASICS

First, think about the money received and paid out. You *receive* money from **donors** or **members**, and you *pay* money to **vendors** and **employees**. Each transaction is grouped with similar transactions into a category, or **general ledger account** (which you will refer to simply as an **account**). For example, power bill or water bill payments may be grouped in an account called *utilities*. All the accounts are compiled into a list called the **Chart of Accounts**. The money may be physically kept in a **bank account**, but it is recorded in a **general ledger account** in your organization's accounting system. The names and information about donors, vendors, employees, and accounts are each stored in their own lists. **Lists** are the foundation of the QBO program. Accurate financial reports depend on your understanding of how lists work, and how to set them up and use them correctly. This isn't nearly as confusing as it may sound.

Open the sample company and you will see a screen like this one.

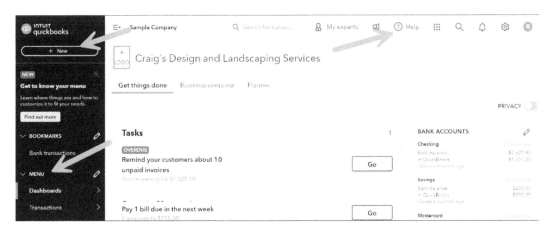

To the left is the Navigation Bar where you will find the menu for **Transactions, Sales, Expenses, Payroll,** and **Reports.** I will refer to this side menu as the **MENU** throughout the book. The **+NEW** on the upper left corner will be the starting point for most of your day-to-day transactions. At the top right are buttons for **Search** (magnifying glass), **Help, Apps** (9 dots), **Notifications** (bell), **Gear,** and your **Account** (circle with initial). The **Gear** icon at the top right to access any of the lists: **Chart of Accounts, Products and Services, Classes, Payment Methods,** etc.

When you go to the QBO **Home** screen, you will have a couple of options on what to see first. QBO offers the Accountant View called **Getting things done** tab (see above illustration) and the Business View on the **Business overview** tab. The Accountant View is designed to take you quickly to transactions that need to be reviewed, categorized, or paid, while the Business overview allows you to quickly see your expected cash flow, profit and loss and unpaid invoices.

 *Click on the three bars at the top left of the screen, to hide the left menu for a full screen effect anywhere in the system.*

To easily see the differences, simply click on the **Getting things done** tab and then the **Business overview** tab in the sample company. When you are ready to set up your own organization's file, go to the **Gear** icon in the upper right corner.

A box will pop up and at the bottom, it will say *"You're viewing QuickBooks in Business view (or Accountant view)."* To the right, in blue letters, it will say *Switch to Accountant view (or Business view)*. Once you select the letters in blue, it will change the home screen and keep it every time you open the system.

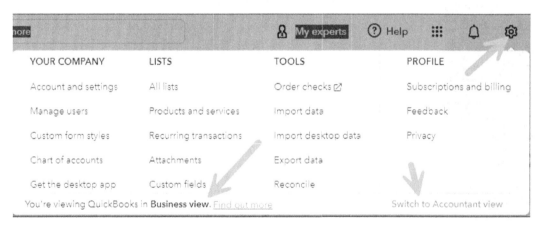

The **Gear** also allows you to access your company settings, preferences, lists, etc. I will cover these in detail as you set up the company file and learn how to enter transactions. But for now, let's go through the **MENU** on the left side of the screen.

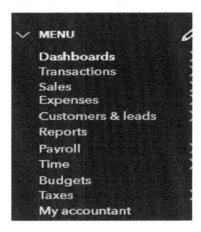

By clicking on the small pencil icon, you can hide any of these options you don't need. For example, if you aren't using QuickBooks Payroll or Time, you may wish to take them off the menu. Above the **MENU** is **BOOKMARKS**. By selecting the pencil icon next to it, you may select pages to have at the top for easy access and then drag them to the order you like to work.

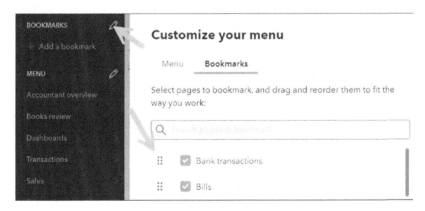

Dashboards will take you back to your home page. **Transactions** takes you to your banking feeds (i.e., checks and deposits downloaded from your bank) to categorize deposits or checks, to any apps you may have connected to QBO, to receipts you have uploaded and need to match to credit card or bank transactions, and much more.

Sales is where you will find lists of donors, their invoices, and the list of Products & services (the items you bill donors). It also shows you overdue invoices, allows you to create new donors, and new invoices. **Expenses** lists vendors, independent contractors, bills and expenses as well as track business mileage. The menus have similar layouts and functionality. I'll use **Sales** as an example. To access, go to the **Navigation Bar** on the left of the home screen and click on *Sales, All Sales.*

From this screen, you will see colored blocks showing you money owed by your donors and what has been recently paid. You can also select *New transaction* and input an invoice, payment, sales receipt, credit memo, etc. This screen also allows you to click *Receive Payment* to easily add a payment from a donor or *Edit* to revise the invoice.

Below that, you can sort the transactions by type, date, or customer. Click on the other tabs to see more detailed information on Customers, Invoices, or Products. Then go to the **Expenses** list and play around there.

Back to the **Menu** list, you will also see **Payroll, Time, Budgets, Taxes,** etc. Check those out at your leisure-I'll be taking you through all of them in detail later in the book.

 *If you get ever get lost in the system, you can always go back to the main screen by clicking on the QB icon in the left **Menu**.*

C. FIND AND CORRECT POSTED TRANSACTIONS

Finding previously posted transactions is easy in QBO. The **Search** box at the top includes a magnifying glass icon that allows you to. If you click on the magnifying glass a list of the most **Recent Transactions** appears. Double click any listed transaction to view the original entry where any corrections can be made. Remember to save any corrections made to the transaction.

You can search transactions, donors, employees, vendors, or reports in this area. Simply type in the name you are looking for.

Double click any listed transaction to view the original entry. Corrections can then be made. Remember to save any adjustments.

You can also get to original transactions by running reports (see Chapter 12). From any report, double clicking on a number to get to the entry screen. You may see me refer to this as "drilling down" on a report.

D. USING QBO HELP

In the top right corner of the QBO screen, you will find the help icon.

Click this icon and enter any phrase to find answers and "how to" instructions on the fly. This is a great resource, but you may need to reword your request a few times before getting the answer you need. You can also call QBO or a ProAdvisor accountant/bookkeeper for help.

If you like to use keyboard shortcuts, use [ctrl] [alt] and [?] to pull up a screen with a list of them It lists your Company ID, which is useful if you have to call into QuickBooks for help. You can also access it by going to Gear, My Company, Additional information.

E. LISTS AND TRANSACTION ENTRY SCREENS

QuickBooks uses lists to fill out transactions. You must let QBO know who a donor is via the **Customer List** and what revenue and bank accounts it should go to via the **Chart of Account List**. To access **All lists**, go to the *Gear* icon.

Each time you enter a donation or pay a bill, you will see a **Transaction Entry Screen**, so I'd like to familiarize you with the format of the system before you get into the details.

The transaction entry screens are designed to look like the forms used in businesses. The fields in these forms are populated by the information set up in the **Lists**. To open a transaction screen, click on the *+New* at the top left side of the home screen.

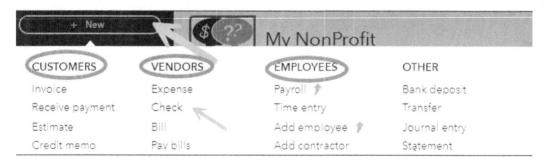

Now you can select the type of transaction you would like to enter. We'll use a check for our example.

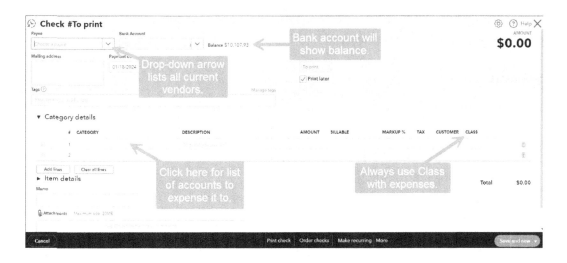

There are drop-down menus for **Payee, Bank Account, Category,** and **Class** (though if you are in the test drive company, you probably won't see the **Class** column). You can also begin typing a name in the respective field, and QBO will automatically populate the field from names found in that list. Finish the transaction by entering the dollar amount and *Save and new.* Close out this screen by clicking on the *X* in the upper right-hand corner.

All transaction entry screens in QuickBooks work in the same basic way. There are fields with drop-down menus for every transaction. As you read this book, play with the test company to become more comfortable with the relationship between lists and transaction entry.

Anytime you see a small gear icon on a transaction screen, you can click on it to change/delete boxes on the forms.

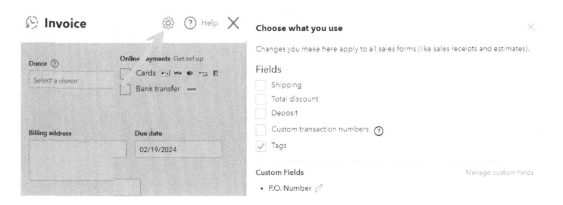

I recommend playing around with the different icons you see, so you can make the system work more efficiently for you.

Summary

In this chapter you learned how to get around QuickBooks Online including:

- The layout of the program
- QuickBooks terminology
- How to find and correct posted transactions
- How to use the Help function and shortcut keys
- How to navigate the lists and transaction entry screens

Remember:
*For **Transactions** (invoices, bills, payments) go to the **+New** icon in the upper left corner.*
*For **Account settings, Lists,** and to do the not-everyday things (import/export data, budgets, reconciliations) go to the **Gear** icon.*
*For **Summaries** of all transactions, check out the **Menu**.*

In Chapter 3, you will be setting up the files and settings to make QBO work most efficiently for your organization.

3

SETTING UP YOUR ORGANIZATION FILE

A. REQUIRED INFORMATION

I t is time to set up your nonprofit or church with QBO. (Note: If the organization is already set up, you can skip to Chapter 5 to learn to work with transactions, but you may want to review this section to see if you can improve your current system.) To get started, you'll need to pull together some data. Below is the basic information you will need to design the data file. A more complete list of information needed to set up the system is on the next page.

1. *Nonprofit's legal name and address*
2. *Federal Employer Identification Number (EIN)*
3. *First month of accounting year—usually January*
4. *Type of tax return—990, 990 EZ, or 990-N, if any*
5. *Chart of accounts—(more details about this in Chapter 4)*

B. CREATING A QBO ACCOUNT

To create and set up your QuickBooks Online account, go to quickbooks.intuit.com/online. This will bring up a screen like this one:

1. Before You Start Checklist

Here is a list of items you will need to set up QuickBooks for your church or nonprofit.

Setting up the Organization File

☐	Legal name and address of the organization
☐	Federal EIN
☐	First month of the accounting year (usually January)
☐	Name of your organization's annual income tax form if applicable

Completing Lists and Entering Balances
Chart of Accounts

☐	Names, numbers, and descriptions for the Chart of Accounts
☐	Financial statements as of the end of the prior year
☐	Trial balances as of the QuickBooks start date
☐	List of programs and grants (for the Class List)
☐	Bank, credit card, and loan account numbers and data
☐	Value of assets (original cost and accumulated depreciation)

Member and Grants Information

☐	Donors' names, addresses, email, etc.
☐	Grant documents
☐	Outstanding invoices or dues as of your organization's transition to QuickBooks start date

Vendor Information

☐	Vendor names, addresses, other contact information
☐	List of 1099 vendors and their tax ID numbers
☐	List of outstanding bills as of your QuickBooks start date

Other Information

☐	Employee names and contact information
☐	Volunteer names and responsibilities

If you want to try it free for 30 days, click on the Chat with sales. But if they are running a special, you probably will not get the discount if you choose the trial first. You will need to select the **+New** or **Advanced** version. The less expensive options do not allow the use of Classes which we need to track funds. If you were able to buy a subscription through Techsoup.org, please follow their directions to log in. Otherwise, follow these instructions.

You will be directed to create your user ID and password using an email address.

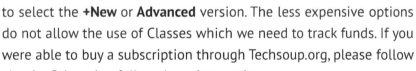

> *The email account used to create the account will be designated as the* ***master administrator****. If possible, use an email attributed to the organization (i.e. treasurer@yournonprofit.org) that can be used by others if you leave your position.*

Once you've filled in the required information, QBO will create your account. Check your email for a confirmation notice. Click Confirm my Intuit account's email address to complete the registration.

A screen will appear asking for more information about your organization.

If you are switching from QuickBooks Desktop, the system will take you through the necessary steps. I've also detailed the process in the section of this chapter following this one. Next it will ask what tasks you plan to do in QuickBooks.

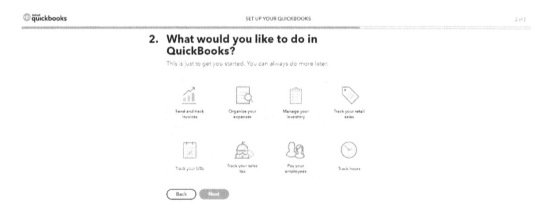

Don't worry if you aren't sure which of these you'll need. You can always turn the features on later. Complete the rest of the screens and you are ready to get to work. In the next section, I'll explain how to move your existing QuickBooks desktop data to QBO. If you are brand new to QuickBooks and will be starting your accounting fresh from this point, grab a cup of tea, and I'll meet you back in Section D.

Some of the screens shown throughout the book may look different than those you will see on your computer. Intuit (the company that makes QBO) frequently changes the look of the screens. The information required will still be basically the same.

C. EXPORTING EXISTING QUICKBOOKS DESKTOP DATA TO QBO

If you are currently using a QuickBooks Desktop (Pro, Premier, or Nonprofit versions, 2008 or later) company, you don't have to start your accounting from scratch to move to QBO. It only takes a few steps to export your historical company and transaction data to QuickBooks Online. Before exporting your data, however, you must do some preparation.

1. Run Reports in Desktop Version

Before you start the export process, it's a good idea to run and print some basic reports. You will use these reports to verify that your data has been converted correctly. I suggest you publish a year-to-date Profit & Loss (income) statement, and a Balance Sheet dated the day of the conversion. I'd also run a general ledger report for the last fiscal year and save it as a pdf file instead of printing it, as it will probably be a large file. The general ledger can be found in the desktop versions under **Reports, Accountant & Taxes, General Ledger.**

It's also good to know where you left off with your transaction entry in the desktop version. Write down the last check number, the last bill, the last donation, and the last deposit you entered. This keeps you from getting confused and duplicating entries into the new system.

2. Export Desktop Company File to QuickBooks Online

Back up your desktop company file and then you can now export the desktop company file to QBO. Keep in mind that the computer where your software is found must be connected to the internet to perform this task.

First log into your QBO account. Then in the desktop program, go to the **Home** screen's top menu bar, choose *Company, Export Company File to QuickBooks Online.*

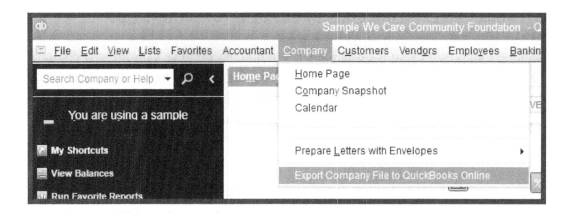

The system then asks how much of your data to bring in. You can bring everything or if it is more than you need, bring over the lists and balances.

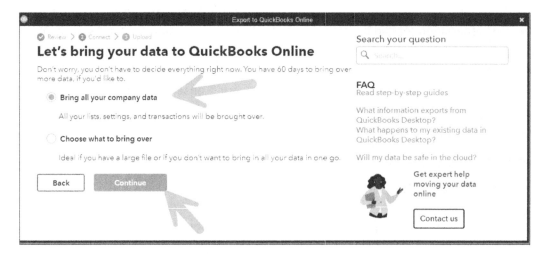

It will ask **"Where do you want to move to?"** and if you are logged into your QBO account, will show it or offer to let you create a new company.

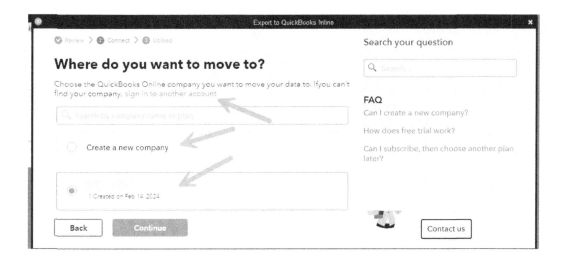

Select *Continue* and a screen showing an **Export** option will appear.

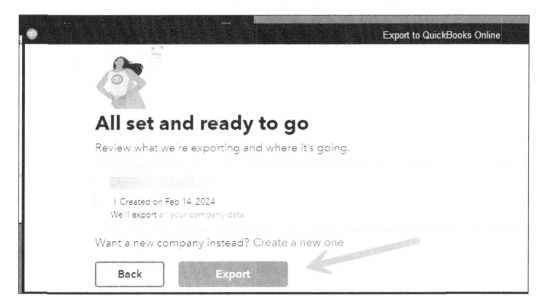

The system will handle the rest. It will take a few minutes for the desktop data to be exported to QBO.

Log into QBO. The system will let you know if the desktop data imported matches what is in QBO.

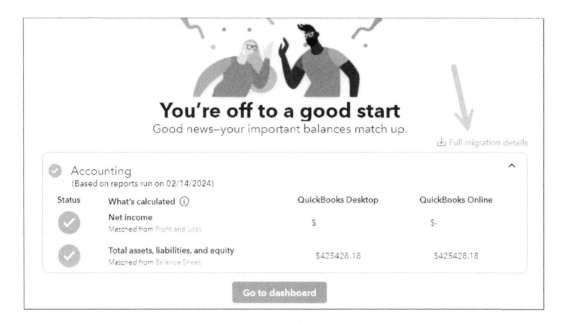

You can also download the **Full migration details** to see a summary of what was sent over. You've got your historical data in the system, so it is time to review and customize the settings.

D. ACCOUNT AND SETTINGS

Settings decide what information will show up on various screens and allow for the flexibility of the system. Due to this flexibility, it is important to understand what each of these options do. To access **Settings**, select the *Gear Icon* in the top right of the home screen. Under **Your Company**, select *Account and Settings*.

Account and Settings will take you to a list of settings categories on the left side of the screen.

The settings found here are global and impact the overall functionality of QBO. I will walk you through the options in many of these categories, and we'll skip the ones you are less likely to use.

1. **Company Settings**

Let's start with *Company* settings located first in the list. Here is where you will add or make updates to your company name, legal name (if different), federal ID number, contact information, and logo. Click on the **Pencil** icon or on the line of any of the areas you wish to edit to key in additional data.

Upload your logo into the system by clicking on the *Company name* section, **+** sign and pointing to the file on your computer. The **Company name** box should be populated with the name you want to show on report headers and forms produced by QBO. If the organization's legal name is different, unclick the **Same as company name** box and enter the legal name. This will be used by the system on payroll and tax forms.

The **Employer ID (EIN)** is your Federal Identification Number. You should be able to find this on your payroll or other reports. You must select *Save* before you can go to the next section on the page. Continue down this screen and enter your contact information and email preferences.

The next block down is the **Tax Form**. Using the pencil to the right, you can change it to *Nonprofit organization (Form 990)* or, if you don't need to file a return (i.e., some churches), select *Not sure/Other/None.* For the **Industry,** type Nonprofit and several options will be offered.

2. Usage

This tab shows you how close you are to any of the QuickBooks limits on accounts or classes. and gives you the option to upgrade.

3. Sales Settings

The next item on the left-hand menu is **Sales.** This screen allows you to customize options related to how the money your organization receives is recorded. Just keep in mind that, for our purposes, sales are actually donations, dues, and contributions for your organization. You won't change much here but pay attention to **Customize** and **Messages** for sales (donation) receipts and membership dues invoices.

Click the *Customize look and feel* button to view and customize form templates. You will arrive at the *Custom Form Styles* list which allows you to create customized invoices and receipts. You may want to create a *New style* (form template) for each type of collections to make, like dues, donations, or pledges.

Select *Edit* to reach a form template. As you have seen on the other QBO screens, the left side will have the menu tabs. Each template allows you to edit the **Style, Appearance, Header, Activity Table,** and **Footer** for an invoice or receipt. You can set the color scheme, rename fields, and change the layout of your forms. Select *Save* to get back to Home page.

If you click on the pencil icon next to **Messages**, you will be taken to a screen to customize the generic email messages set up for Invoices (Pledges) and Sales Receipts.

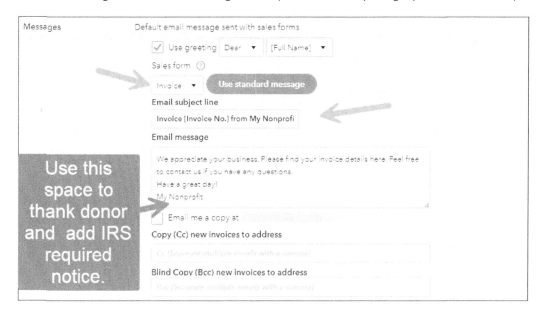

4. **Expenses/Expenditures Settings**

Let's go back to the **Settings**. Click on Gear, *Your Company, Account and Settings*. This time you are going to *Expenditures* settings. The **Expenditures** screen under **Account and Settings** allows you to customize options related to how money paid out is recorded. Here you will make choices about what fields are available on expense and purchase forms.

Turn the **Bills and expenses** options to **On.** If you have grants and need to track expenditures by grantee, turn on the next two items. (I'll explain this in more detail in Chapters 5 and 8.) Turn **Purchase orders** off unless your organization currently uses them. This is also the area you can customize your default **Messages** on your purchase orders. Now, let's look at **Payments** settings.

5. **Payment Settings**

The payment settings screen is only used if you choose to sign up with Intuit to accept payments directly through emailed invoices or mobile devices. There is an added cost for this service. In Chapter 8, I'll explain the cost and benefits for these.

6. **Advanced Settings**

The last tab is titled **Advanced**. I want you to understand these options as they have a significant impact on the accounting.

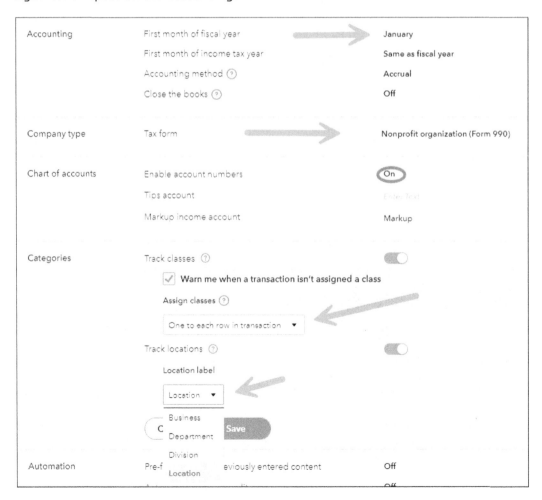

As you have done previously, double click on any section or click the pencil to make edits. Remember to select *Save* after your changes to each section and *Done* when you are finished with **Advanced** settings, as shown on the following page.

In the *Accounting* section, you will select the first month of your organization's fiscal year and accounting method. Usually, the fiscal year and the calendar year are the same, but if your organization closes its books on June 30 each year instead of December 31, use July for the **First month of fiscal year.** As a small nonprofit or church, you probably don't really have to worry about the income tax year.

Accounting method determines when you record income and expenses. For small organizations, the **Cash** method is more common. Larger organizations and those who must send their financial statements to large donors usually use the **Accrual** method. QBO allows you to change the accounting method on reports easily.

You can also set a **Close the books** date to keep users from recording data in an earlier accounting period. I'll show you how to use this in Chapter 14, but for now, let's leave it off.

In the **Company type** section, you will choose the tax form for your organization, most likely Form 990. If you are a religious organization, you may not have to file any tax return at all.

For the **Chart of Accounts** section, it is important to **Enable account numbers**. I will go into detail about that in the next chapter.

The Categories block includes the options to track classes and locations. It is crucial you select *Track classes* to account for nonprofit programs, funds, and grants. You will also want to the *Warn me when a transaction isn't assigned a class.* You may choose whether to assign the class to the entire transaction or select by line item.

Locations are a way for QBO to track separate departments, businesses, or locations. They can be used with Classes for more flexibility. Select **Track locations,** if desired, and choose a *Location Label.*

Automation allows you to have the system take care of prefilling forms. Turn these on to try if you'd like, but no you can turn them off any time.

Projects are one of the newest ways QuickBooks allows you to track data. Go ahead and turn it on. I'll explain how to use it in a later chapter.

Let's skip the **Time Tracking** and **Currency** sections, assuming you aren't billing hours or working in multiple currencies. If so, please explore these options, but they are beyond the scope of this book.

The next block is **Other preferences**. Besides changing the date and number formats, you can change the **Customer label** from "customer" to "donor" or "member" depending on the main group your organization receives money from. Also, turn on the **Warn if duplicate check number is used**. Click on the **X** in the upper right corner to exit.

7. **Other Options under YOUR COMPANY**

Next under *Gear, YOUR COMPANY,* are several other options I'll be covering later in the book. With **Mange Users***,* you can add users with different privileges and accountants. **Custom form styles** allows you to upload your logo and make your Pledge statements personalized. Both will be covered in Chapter 15. The **Chart of Accounts** is covered in the next chapter. **Get the desktop app** allows you to download an app to your computer to save logging in time and gives you the ability to open multiple windows on QBO at a time. You will find that immensely helpful. Just follow the instructions to download.

The **Additional information** will give you a box with your Company ID (particularly useful if you have to call QuickBooks for help) and keyboard shortcuts.

E. LISTS

From the *Gear*, you will also see **LISTS**. This is where you can access all the lists of things in QBO, i.e., **Recurring transactions, Classes, Attachments** to transactions, **Custom fields**, etc.

F. TOOLS

Under *Gear, TOOLS,* you will find things to help with the things you don't do every day. For example, you can **Order checks**, **Import** and **Export data, Reconcile** accounts, enter **Budgets**, see the **Audit log**, use **SmartLook** so the QuickBooks support desk can see your computer, and track any open issues you have with the support desk under the **Resolution center**. Look around this area so you know where to go when necessary.

G. PROFILE

The final area under **Gear** is **PROFILE**. Here you can find your **Subscriptions and billing**, offer **Feedback,** and see the **Privacy notice. Subscriptions and billing** will show you the details and options about your QuickBooks Online account including your **Company ID**.

Use this number anytime you contact QuickBooks customer support. This screen also shows you any additional services you have enrolled in, like **Payroll** or **Payments** (to accept credit cards and bank drafts from donors).

Summary:

In this chapter, you learned the following:

- What information is needed
- How to create a QBO account
- How to export your existing QuickBooks Desktop Data into QBO
- How to set your preferences in Account and Settings to make the system work most efficiently for you
- Familiarized you with the **Gear** functions

Now it is time to learn how to set up a chart of accounts.

4

WHAT IS THE CHART OF ACCOUNTS?

A. DESIGNING THE CHART OF ACCOUNTS

Now it is time to determine our chart of accounts. This is the listing of all the accounts used to record transactions. The accounts are then used for generating your financial reports. For now, don't worry about programs or grants; you only want to concentrate on the individual accounts where you will be posting transactions.

If you are currently using a chart of accounts that works for your organization, you may wish to design something similar, but first read this chapter so you understand how QBO uses the information for both transactions and reporting. I'd also recommend that you have an accountant or member who knows accounting requirements review any chart of accounts you are planning to use to make sure it will work for your organization.

The best way to design a chart of accounts is to first consider your reporting requirements. If you file a tax return (990 or 990EZ), you will want to be certain you are tracking expenses that can easily be summarized in those categories. If you have a national or parent organization you report to, look at their reporting requirements to see what should be included.

And try to keep it as **simple** as possible. I don't like to use the QBO recommended accounts unless you scan through the list and remove all the extras. I would discourage you from using the Unified Chart of Accounts (UCOA) for nonprofits unless your organization is large and needs most of those accounts. My website www.AccountantBesideYou.com has my recommended charts of accounts for several different types of nonprofits and religious organizations. If your organization has similar programs, consider using one of these as your guideline.

In designing your chart of accounts, you need to understand how accountants define the distinct types of accounts. One of the best explanations I have seen comes from the *Small Non-Profit QuickBooks Primer* by Poppy Davis, CPA. An excerpt is on the next page.

Assets stick around.   ***Expenses   go   away.***
If you buy a stove for the kitchen, it will stick around, so it is an asset. If the stove breaks and you repair it, that is an expense (the repair man goes away, the stove is back to working like it is supposed to).

Income is yours.   ***Liabilities belong to others.***
So if you receive a donation or a grant to serve meals to people, it is income, but if you borrow money from the bank to build a new kitchen, it is a liability.

Net Assets are what is left over for you

QuickBooks does not use the proper non-profit name "net equity," instead it uses **Beginning Balance Equity** (the Net Assets the first time you enter information to set the business up) and **Retained Earnings** (the change in Net Assets over time).

B. NUMBERING STRUCTURE

I strongly recommend you use account numbers. QBO does not require account numbers, but you will severely limit your reporting options if you do not use them. The numbers can be anything up to seven digits, but unless you have an overly complex system, I recommend starting with just four or five. QBO automatically sorts the chart of accounts by account type and runs reports according to this sorting.

Assets are sorted by:

- Bank Account
- Accounts Receivable
- Other Current Assets
- Fixed Assets
- Other Assets

Liabilities are sorted by:

- Accounts Payable
- Credit Card

- Other Current Liability
- Long-Term Liability

 *A **current asset** or **liability** is due or used within a year. A **long-term asset** or **liability** is available or due in more than a year. For example, a pledge made for the next year is a current asset, but a capital campaign contribution due in five years is a long-term asset.*

All the other accounts are sorted by number. Therefore, if you have numbers out of sequence with the type, you cannot view your chart of accounts in numerical order. This will become much clearer in Chapter 12 on Reports.

 1000s—Assets: bank accounts, receivables, computers, etc.
2000s—Liabilities: accounts payable, payroll, loans, etc.
3000s—Net Assets: with donor restrictions and without donor restrictions.
4000s—Donations and Support: dues, donations, bequests, capital campaigns, endowments etc.
5000s—Earned Revenues: program service fees, membership dues, fundraisers, interest, fixed asset sales.
6000s—Operating/Functional Expenses: facilities, salaries, program costs, etc.
7000s—Non-operating Expenses: extraordinary repairs, depreciation, etc.
8000s—Ask My Accountant: a place to record transactions you don't know what to do with. This is then reviewed by your accountant on a regular basis and cleared up.

Within the above, consider using the ranges below as a basic recommendation for the balance sheet asset accounts:

1101-1199	Cash and investments
1201-1299	Undeposited monies (I'll explain this in Chapter 8)
1301-1399	Receivables—amounts owed to you
1401-1499	Prepaid assets—this can be insurance, postage, etc.
1501-1699	Available for current assets categories in the future
1701-1799	Building, real estate, and the related depreciation

WHAT IS THE CHART OF ACCOUNTS?

1801-1899	Available for long-term assets categories in the future

1901-1999   Other long-term assets.

As you can see, this gives you at least 99 accounts under each of the categories. Use the same concepts for the Liability accounts in the 2000 level and Net Assets/Equity accounts in the 3000 range.

Consider how you would like to see your expenses grouped together. Using the ranges above, you may also wish to have sub-ranges. For example, the facility costs may be in 6000-6399, personnel expenses in 6400-6599, and program expenses from 6600-6999. As you need to add accounts within a range, consider adding them by 10s or 100s so you will have space between accounts. For clubs and smaller organizations, using four-digit account numbers should be sufficient.

Reporting requirements to governing agencies, grantors, and the government will determine how to set up your income and expenses accounts. The first thing I want you to look at is the tax returns or annual reports your organization filed last year. If your organization did not file a return and you wonder if you should, please contact your local accountant or go to www.irs.gov for filing requirements. Due to the myriad of laws and the differing types of organizations and organizations, this book does not offer any tax advice.

If you will be filing IRS Form 990EZ, the income requirements as of the writing of this book are:

1. Contributions, gifts, grants, and similar amounts
2. Program service revenue
3. Membership dues and assessments
4. Investment income
5. Gross amount from sale of assets other than inventory
6. Gaming and fundraising events
7. Gross sales of inventory
8. Other revenue.

The expense requirements are:

1. Grants and similar amounts paid
2. Benefits paid to or for donors

3. Salaries, other compensation, and employee benefits
4. Professional fees and other payments to independent contractors
5. Occupancy, rent, utilities, and maintenance
6. Printing, publications, postage, and shipping
7. Other expenses.

This would be the minimum number of income statement accounts required for Form 990EZ. If you file Form 990, a Statement of Revenue and a Statement of Functional Expenses will also be needed. You will therefore need a few more accounts:

1. Federated campaigns
2. Related organizations
3. Government grants (contributions)
4. Noncash contributions.

All the income will have to be designated on the 990 as Related function revenue, Unrelated business revenue, or Revenue excluded from tax. In Chapter 5, I will show you how to set up programs to help with that information.

There are more expense-reporting requirements on Form 990.

1. Grants paid must show payments to government and organizations separate from individuals.
2. Grants paid to organizations, governments, or individuals outside of the US are accounted for separately.
3. Compensation to current officers, directors, trustees, and key employees is listed separately, as is pension plans and contributions and other employee benefits.
4. Expenses are broken out in more detail.
5. All expenses are then designated into one of three categories:
   a. Program Services
   b. Management & General
   c. Fundraising.

The National Center for Charitable Statistics supports the UCOA, the Unified Chart of Accounts, for nonprofit organizations. If you are large enough to file Form 990 and report to outside organizations, this may be a practical choice for you. But because the chart of accounts was designed for large nonprofits with numerous activities, there will be many excess accounts you probably won't need.

At AccountantBesideYou.com, I have sample charts of accounts for several types of nonprofits available to purchase. The first one is a simplified version of the UCOA geared toward less complex nonprofits, but still has sufficient accounts to handle the 990 or 990EZ. Next, I have included a chart of accounts based on the ASAE (American Society of Association Executives), standard for an association's records. There are also sample charts for PTAs, civic clubs, scouting groups, and private schools. Many deviate from the numbering system I show below, but they are based on their specific industries' recommendations. My recommended chart of accounts for churches and other religious organizations is designed for small and growing churches as a starting point.

C. NAMING THE ACCOUNTS

Once you have figured out your numbering system, you need to determine how you are going to name the accounts. This sounds extremely basic, but if you aren't careful, you may have accounts called "Postage and Mailing," "Postage," "Post," etc., which should all be combined. To keep things simple, have a policy that significant words are written out with no punctuation marks, and ampersands (&) are used instead of the word "and." If you already have a naming protocol, by all means use it.

 For now, don't worry about setting up accounts for individual programs or grants. I'll explain how to set those up in Chapter 5.

D. BUILDING THE CHART OF ACCOUNTS

It's time to input your chart of accounts. Here I'll show you how to set up the accounts from scratch, but if you like to save time typing, go to accountantbesideyou.com and buy a download of my recommended the chart of accounts file for your type of organization. You can also start with the QBO default chart of accounts and delete any accounts you don't need and rename the others. You'll simply upload the file and merge or delete any duplicate accounts. I'll explain how to merge and delete an account on page 50.

You can find the **Chart of Accounts** by going to the *Gear* icon at the top right corner of the screen and click on *Chart of Accounts* under **Your Company**.

You can also access the accounts under *Gear, LISTS, All lists* or select *Transactions, Bank Transactions, Chart of Accounts tab* from the Main Menu on the left side of the homepage.

Arriving at the Chart of Accounts, you will see a list of accounts QBO has created based on the industry choices you made during company creation. Because you selected **Enable and Show Account Numbers** under the **Chart of Accounts** section of **Advanced Settings**, the system automatically inserted a blank number column of fields for each account. Note that account numbers are limited to a maximum of seven digits.

To begin entering and renaming accounts, click on the pencil just above the list of accounts. This opens the batch edit function which allows you to change only account numbers and rename accounts, not to add or delete.

Remember to click *Save* when done. Next, you will learn how to add and edit accounts.

E. SYSTEM GENERATED ACCOUNTS

QBO automatically generates some accounts that they will not let you delete, but you can edit the titles. The most important one you need to address is **Retained Earnings.** This is the account that QBO automatically moves the prior year's profit or loss into. You will want to rename it to be your general fund or **Without Donor Restrictions Net Assets or Without Donor Restrictions-General Fund** by scrolling down on the batch edit page. You will not want to change anything but the title.

F. ADDING NEW ACCOUNTS

You can add one new account at a time by going to the *Gear, Your Company, Chart of Accounts* and selecting *New* at the top right corner of the screen. This will take you to the account entry screen.

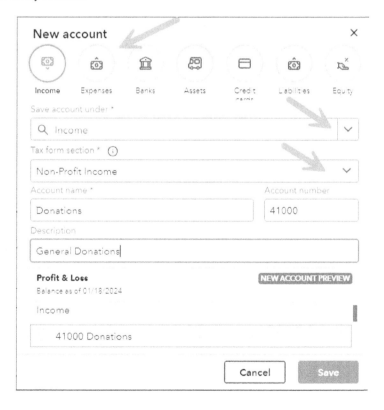

The first thing you need to do is decide the Account Type which defines each account's purpose. These are shown in circles with icons. As I discussed earlier in the chapter, QBO needs to know what the account's purpose is to use it properly. If you change the **Account Type**, there will be corresponding changes in the options from the drop-down menu under **Save account under.** The **Tax form section** allows you to further define the account. In this example, I am adding an income account for donations and assigning an account number. The system then shows me where that account will appear in the financial statements.

If I was adding a bank account, I would select the circle with **Banks** under it. Then I would select the drop-down arrow and select Bank Accounts, or I could have it be a sub-account under another bank. For example, if you have several checking accounts, but want to have a condensed balance sheet showing only the sum of all the checking accounts, you will set up a Checking **Parent Account.** Then each of the individual checking accounts would be subaccounts. Subaccounts allow you to track your accounts with more detail and give you more reporting flexibility.

The **Tax form** section has the option to say if it is savings, checking, money market, etc.

Enter an Account **Number** in the appropriate field. Remember they are limited to a maximum of seven digits. Under **Description**, you may wish to add a note to remind you what this account is used for.

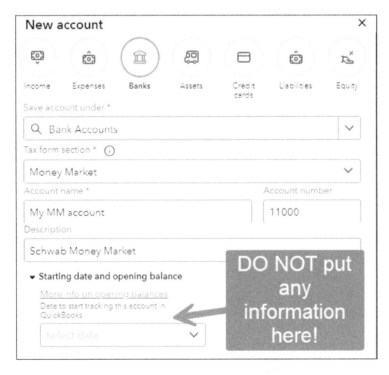

There is an arrow labeled **Starting date and opening balance**. *Do not use this!* You will be putting the opening balances in as a journal entry. In accounting, every journal entry must balance the left side of the entry with the right side. Using a journal entry to record your beginning balances is an important way to make certain that your system balances correctly from the start. Select the drop-down arrow next to **Save** to select *Save and New* and continue adding accounts.

To easily pull up your electricity costs separate from your gas costs, you may have a parent account called **Utilities** and subaccounts (using the Save account under area) named **Electricity** and **Gas**. You could then run reports summing up all utilities or a more detailed report on each of the subaccounts. To use QBO correctly for fund accounting, you need to use subaccounts, as you will see later in this chapter.

If you need to prepare reports using GAAP (Generally Accepted Accounting Principles), you may wish to set up sub-accounts under Net Assets with Donor Restrictions for Endowments or other restrictions.

 Input your "parent" accounts first and then you can easily put subaccounts in the "Save account under" section. For example, enter Utilities first, then Gas, Water, Electric, etc.

G. TRACKING RESTRICTED CASH

As was discussed in the first chapter, one of QBO's limitations for nonprofits is that it does not handle fund accounting by separate funds. If your organization uses separate bank accounts for donor-restricted versus without donor restrictions cash, then the cash will be tracked by bank accounts. But most organizations have one checking account that all transactions go through.

1. Using Custom Reports to Track Restricted Cash

There are two different ways for you to track the restricted versus unrestricted cash in a single checking account. The first (and my recommended) approach is to set up your general ledger account for checking based the individual bank account (i.e., Account number 1010=Checking Account). You will then design a report to show the amount of restricted cash versus unrestricted cash within the account. This approach works as long as you use classes for your programs and funds. Chapter 5 will explain the use of classes, and in Chapter 14, I will walk you through the process of setting up the restricted cash report.

2. Multiple Subaccounts for Cash

In the second method, you will need to set up subaccounts for any bank account that has both restricted and unrestricted cash. For this approach, set up two subaccounts under each of your checking and investment accounts: Without Donor Restrictions, and With Donor Restrictions. When you record payments or receipts, you will always use one of these three, not the parent account. The reconciliation will be done in the parent account, which will have all the transactions. I don't recommend this approach as you have to be very conscientious to get the right subaccount each time you write a check.

You must be careful about not accidentally posting items to the parent accounts. This is important as any cash posted directly to the parent will not be reflected in either the restricted or the unrestricted cash.

This approach allows you to see unrestricted versus restricted cash balances anytime you open the account list but requires more attention as you enter transactions. Each time you enter a bill, deposit money, or transfer cash, you will need to assure you have selected the correct subaccount.

H. UPLOAD A CHART OF ACCOUNTS

Starting out with a relevant chart of accounts is crucial to any organization. If you are using a chart of accounts from a parent organization or have bought one of the charts of accounts downloads available at www.AccountantBesideyou.com it is easy to upload it into QBO. (Excel must already be on your computer). Download the file and save it to your computer where you can easily find it. Now we are ready to upload the file.

In QBO, select *Chart of Accounts* from the *Gear, My Company, Chart of Accounts*. In the top right corner of the **Chart of Accounts** screen, select the downward arrow to the right of the *New* button and click *Import*.

The system will let you know the maximum number of accounts you can import for your subscription level.

On the **Import Accounts** screen, select *Browse* to find the file you just saved on your computer. (If you are wanting to import a chart of accounts from another source, you can select **Download a sample file** to get the correct format.)

This will open the computer's browser. Locate the file on your computer and double click it. The **Import Accounts** will reappear with the Excel file listed. Select *Next* at the bottom right-hand corner of your screen.

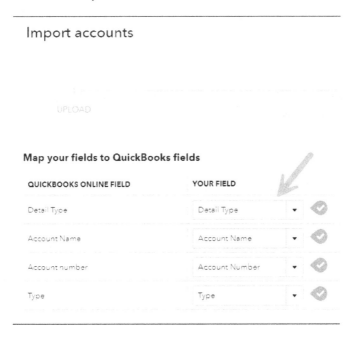

Here you will map the fields from your spreadsheet to the **QuickBooks Online Fields**. **Your Field** options are the headings from the spreadsheet. In other words, you are matching the spreadsheet data to the related QBO fields. Click *Next* to continue.

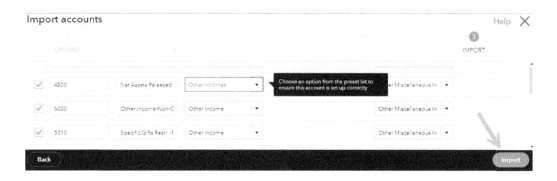

The final screen will detail how QBO will import the accounts. Because QBO sometimes changes their terminology, i.e., Expenses vs Expenditures, so you may see some errors. Use the drop-down arrows to find the correct account type. The **Type** must be correct before the **Detail Type** will show correct. Scroll through the list and make any necessary changes using the drop-down arrows by each box. Anything highlighted in red will not be imported, so you need to change the type or unselect the account. Unselect any accounts that you don't need by deselecting the arrows to the left of the account.

 If you import an acount that is already set up in QuickBooks, it will show in red and not import. Just deselect it and continue.

When you are satisfied with the list, select *Import*. There may be errors if any of the new accounts are already in your company file. Don't worry, duplicate accounts will not be added. To verify the import, go to *Menu, Transactions, Chart of Accounts* and view your new Chart of Accounts.

I. ENTER CHART OF ACCOUNTS (COA)

If you did not upload your accounts, take your list and start entering each account. It is easiest if you go down the list, so the parent accounts are input before the subaccounts. Don't worry about messing something up with your chart of accounts. After you've input all the accounts, I am going to show you how to edit, delete, or deactivate.

 Plan on an entire afternoon for this process.
This is the most tedious step.

J. EDITING, DELETING (DEACTIVATING), AND MERGING ACCOUNTS

1. Edit Accounts

You have very carefully input your chart of accounts or have uploaded the file from my website, and now you need to check your work. The easiest way to edit your account list is to **print** it out or use the **Batch Edit** function. Go to *Gear, Your Company, Chart of Accounts* and select the printer icon to print. Now you will see a listing of all accounts and their types.

QBO has added an especially useful feature called **Batch Edit**. You will find it on the Chart of accounts page by selecting the *small pencil* icon on the upper right side near the printer icon.

The batch edit allows you to quickly scan your COA for missing numbers and wrong or misspelled account names. It will not allow you to change **Account** or **Detail Type** or delete the account. I recommend you go through this list first and make any changes.

If you find anything you would like to change, editing an account is quite easy with QBO. Go to the chart of accounts list, click on the downward arrow found to the right of the account you are editing, and select *Edit* under the drop-down menu.

This will bring up a screen that looks just like the one you used to set up the account. Choose the field you need to edit and make the changes. The only exception relates to the account type which we will discuss next. *Save and Close* when finished.

2. Change Account Type

When QBO creates an account automatically, like Payroll Liabilities, Accounts Receivable, or Accounts Payable, the system will not allow the type to be changed. If you accidentally made an account as an Accounts Receivable type, but it shouldn't have been, you will need to delete the account and reenter it with the correct type. Don't feel bad, however. I do it far more often than I care to admit.

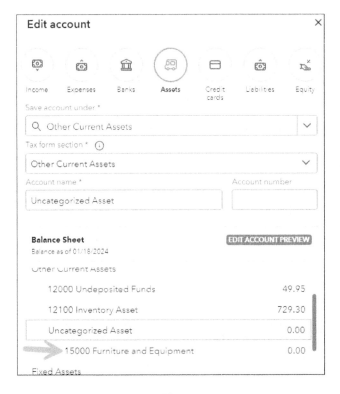

If you need to change the type for a parent account with a subaccount, you will first need to move it from the **Save account under** area.

The account is then no longer a subaccount, and you can change the type, first in the parent, then the subaccount. After you've changed all the types, you will then want to go back and replace the subaccount option in each of the proper accounts.

3. **Delete an Account**

You don't actually delete an account in QBO; you make it inactive. Click on the downward arrow found to the right of the account you are deleting and select *Make inactive* under the drop-down menu.

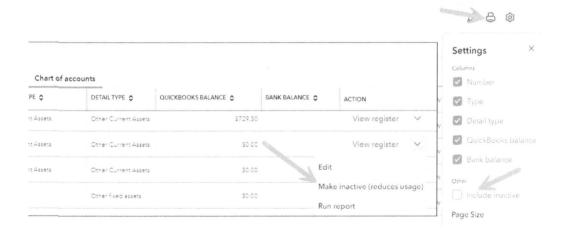

You will then be asked to verify that you really want to do that. If you press **Yes**, the account and its subaccounts will be deactivated. A warning will pop up if you try to make an account inactive that the system automatically generates. It informs you that the system will add that account if it needs it in the future.

I should tell you that making an account inactive does not remove the transactions posted to that account but only removes them from the Chart of Accounts list. You can return the account back to the Chart of Account list by selecting the *Gear* icon on the Chart of Account screen, *Include inactive.*

Previously inactive accounts will then be included in the account list. You will recognize these accounts by the word "deleted" in parentheses after the account name.

Click *Make active* to make the deleted account active again.

If you have a lot of extra accounts, you can delete several at a time using the Batch function on the upper left side of the screen.

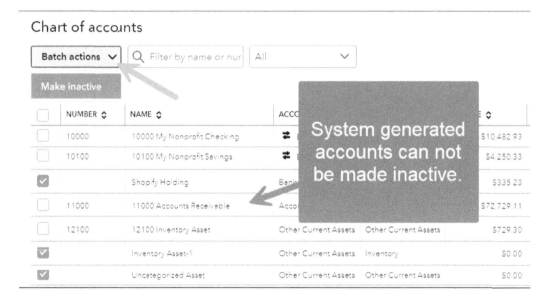

4. **Merging Accounts**

You may have two accounts with similar transactions that really should be in one account. For example, you may have a "Postage" account and a "Postage and Mailing" account. Both accounts contain the same type of transactions and can be merged together in QBO.

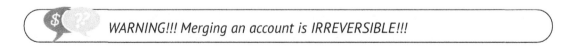

WARNING!!! Merging an account is IRREVERSIBLE!!!

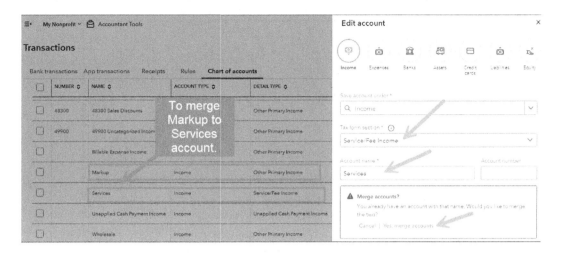

Go to *Gear, Your Company, Chart of Accounts*. Make sure that the accounts you want to merge are at the same sub-level and are the same detail type. If they're not, edit one of the accounts to put it at the same level and give it the same detail type as the other. Select the account whose name you **don't** want to use and click its drop-down arrow under the **Action** column. Select *Edit* and change the account name so that it is exactly the same as the account with which you're merging. Change the Tax form section to match the one you are saving. Click **Save** and **Yes** to confirm that you want to merge the two accounts.

K. BEGINNING BALANCES

Look how much you have accomplished. You've set up the program, defined your settings, and even now have a working Chart of Accounts. Now you need to take the beginning balances for each of the balance sheet accounts and put them in the system. If you have an accountant, ask him for this list. If not, you'll need to get them from your earlier system or calculate them from bank statements and the like.

The beginning balances will be input as a journal entry.

	Debit	Credit
Checking	$ 1,000	
Money Market	3,000	
Building	100,000	
Payroll Taxes Payable		1,000
Mortgage Payable		70,000
Equity—Net Assets without Donor Restriction		30,000
Equity—Temporarily Restricted Net Assets-Smith		1,000
Equity—Unrestricted Net Assets		2,000

Journal entries must always balance. This means all the amounts being coded to assets must equal the amounts coded to liabilities and equity. In journal entries, accountants refer to these as **Debits** and **Credits**. As you can see, the debits and the credits in the entry above both equal $104,000. This is a balanced entry. The equity account (Without Donor Restriction Net Assets that you previously set up) is the offset to make the amounts balance.

I recommend using the last day of your previous accounting year as the date of this entry. You can start using QBO anytime throughout the year but will need to input this year's data to catch up. I'll explain how to do that in Chapters 8 and 9.

Let me step you through the above. In chapter 5, I'll show you how to record journal entries, but first I want you to understand what the entry is recording. The **Checking** and **Money Market** amounts should net to the reconciled balance as of the start date. The **Building** is based on purchase price or value (ask your accountant), and **Mortgage Payable** is the amount you owe the bank. The **Payroll Taxes Payable** is any money not yet paid for taxes or benefits on payroll. I haven't listed Depreciation, because many small nonprofits and churches do not pay taxes and therefore, do not need to depreciate their building or assets. If your reporting requirements to donors or the IRS require it, you will want to include it.

You may have **Accounts Payables** (bills you owe people) or **Accounts Receivables** (money owed to you) as part of your beginning balances. If so, you will need to input them separately by individual donor or vendor and invoice, which I will discuss in Chapters 8 and 9. If you try to input these in the beginning balance entry, QuickBooks will require the amount to go to only one vendor or one customer. Additionally, QuickBooks will not let you post a journal entry with both accounts payable (A/P) and accounts receivable (A/R) data in it.

To record the beginning balances journal entry, you will need another piece of information. Your organization probably has several funds, grants, and programs with designated money in the beginning balances. So, in the next chapter, I'll show you how to organize those.

Summary

In this chapter, we covered the importance of the chart of accounts. Additionally, you learned how to:

- Design the Chart of Accounts
- Determine your numbering and naming structures
- Add new accounts
- Handle restricted cash via custom reports or subaccounts
- Upload a Chart of Accounts
- Add, edit, delete, and merge accounts

Now let's move onto understanding how to use classes to track your funds.

5

HOW DO I TRACK
MY PROGRAMS & FUNDS?

A. USING CLASSES

Throughout the year, your organization may have received money from donors with specific instructions. Sometimes these are formal grants (money given by an organization or government for a specific purpose) and other times they are received from individuals who want the money spent on certain programs. These are referred to as restricted funds, and it is important to track how these dollars are used. As discussed earlier, QBO is not designed to handle the tracking of funds or individual programs within the organization, so you will utilize classes. Classes will be used to track expenses into particular programs, i.e., Education, Worship, Admin and to track donations and the related expenses to specific projects like a grant from Health and Human Services or funds for a Mission Trip.

By using classes, you are able to limit the number of accounts in your chart of accounts and expand your reporting capabilities. For example, most of your organization's programs use supplies. Classes allow you to charge the supplies used (via an account) to several different programs instead of having to set up subaccounts under supplies for each program. Classes are used to track both the revenue and the expenses of a grant.

As you work in the system, every time you see classes, think programs or funds. Before you set up your classes, I'd like you to look at any reporting requirements you have. If you have an audit from last year, study it. If you have a board of directors or governing committee that requires annual or quarterly reports, use them as a good source for the kind of information you may need to track. Review the documents to see what information is required. Nonprofits that file a tax return must designate what money was spent on programs versus administration versus fundraising.

Classes vs. Account Numbers
Account numbers *are used to show specifics on the financial statements, like donations or utilities.*
Classes *are used to allocate the dollars to various programs or funds. For example, if you wanted to charge a literacy program for 20% of the utilities, you would code the expense to the Utilities account with 20% to the Literacy class and the remainder to other classes.*

Additionally, any funds for special purposes or events will need to be set up as classes. For every program you want to report the related expenses (i.e., supplies, postage, donations), a class will need to be set up. Finally, all money restricted either temporarily or permanently should have a class designated.

If a donor or foundation has given money for a grant with a specific purpose, you will need to track the related expenditures. This is where the use of the **Sub-customer** (or sub-donor) and **Projects** options comes in. You learned in Chapter 3 how to change your company preferences from Customers to Donors. From here forward, I will refer to contributors as Donors.

Sub-donors can be linked to only one donor. For those of you familiar with the desktop version of QuickBooks, sub-customers are the equivalents of jobs and allow you to track specific revenue and expenditures related to a donor. For example, if one of your regular donors, Joe Smith, gives your organization an extra $1000 to be used for building a playground, you would set up Joe Smith as the donor and Joe Smith Playground as the sub-donor. You will not set up programs this way because they tend to have numerous donors and related expenses.

 The grant (sub-donor) will also be linked to a fund class. In this chapter, you will be setting up two separate types of classes: program classes and fund classes. The fund classes are necessary to track restricted versus unrestricted funds. The program classes are geared towards understanding program costs.

Here are some guidelines on how to determine which type of class and whether or not you need a Sub-donor.

Description	Program Class	Fund Class	Sub-donors	Project
Is it a program within the organization?	√			
Are there numerous donors?	√			
Do you need to track the expenses with the fund balance?	√	√	√	√
Did the donor specify how the money is to be spent?	√	√	√	√
Is there a single donor?		√	√	√
Will I be required to give the donor an accounting of the funds?			√	√
Is this a large project I'll need more detailed reporting for?				√
Am I billing employees time to the grant?				√

If you answered yes to the last six questions, set up a sub-donor under the donor's name in accounts receivable and/or projects. (More about this is Chapter 6.) If the answer is no, you can simply include those monies with other funds in a fund or program class.

In the next chapter, we will talk about donors and the use of sub-donors and projects to track grants. If you have several grants, you will not want to make a class for each one. Instead, you will assign the sub-donors to the restricted or temporarily restricted class.

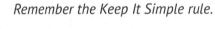

Remember the Keep It Simple rule.

Use as few classes as possible. Utilize Projects and Sub-donors to help limited the number of classes. You can always add more as needed.

B. NAMING OF CLASSES

QBO allows for sub-classes but does not require you to post to the lowest sub-class like you do in the chart of accounts. Therefore, you will want to clearly title your sub-classes, so you know which account the sub-class is associated with. For example, if your primary program is teaching literacy at three different community centers, you may wish to designate a class called 100 Literacy. Then set up sub-classes for locations, i.e., 110 Literacy-Library, 120 Literacy-Senior Center, and 130 Literacy-High School.

QuickBooks shows the classes using a drop-down menu, listing the names in alphanumeric order. I recommend using numbers in front of your class names to keep program classes together and fund classes together.

This also allows you to name the program you will be using the most to show up at the top. For example, you have classes titled Admin, Literacy, and Job Skills, but most of your expenses besides salaries are Admin related. If you were to title the classes 100 Admin, 200 Literacy, etc., then Admin would always be your first option.

Before you start entering the class information, make a list of all the programs you would like to track. I strongly recommend not making this list too long. Do not try to track more detail than you have the need for. For example, you may have a literacy program with a men's focus and a women's focus. If you are only concerned about the cost of the literacy programs in total, use only one class, but if different people are responsible for the expenses of the men's group versus the women's group, use separate classes or sub-classes under a Literacy Programs class. The more detailed you make the classes, the more information you will need to enter when recording the bills, and the more complex your reporting will be.

As another example, here is a possible class list for a private school.

- 100   Administration
- 200   Preschool
- 210   Elementary
- 220   Middle School
- 230   High School
- 310   Extended Day
- 320   After-School Enrichment
- 500   Fundraising
- 600   Scholarships
- 900   Unrestricted Funds
- 910   Donor Restricted Funds

C. ENTERING CLASS LISTS

Now that you have compiled your list, let's input your classes in the system. You will find the *Class List* under the *All lists* option on the gear icon.

Select the **Classes** option in the right-hand column of the next menu. This will bring up the following screen (though yours may be blank).

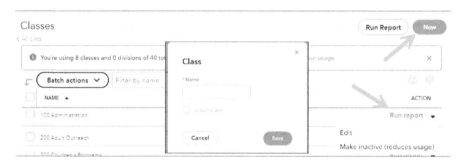

As you can see, this is similar to the screen to add a new account. Select *New* and type in the name of the class you wish to add. If you wish to set up sub-classes, check the *Is sub-class* box. You can then select the down arrow for a list of available classes. Select *Save* to exit.

D. EDITING OR DELETING CLASSES

Once you have your classes entered, you may find you'd like to make some changes. Editing or deleting classes is very simple. Choose *Gear, All Lists, Classes* to open the **Classes List.** For the class you would like to change, click on the down arrow on that class line to select *Edit* or *Delete*. The **Edit** option lets you change the name or sub-class or make it a parent class. The **Delete** option does not actually delete the account—it marks it as inactive and hides it from the list. If you select *Delete,* a pop-up box will ask you to verify that you really want to delete the class.

Similar to accounts, you can bring a deleted class back into the list from the *Classes Gear Icon* just above the class list.

Click *Include inactive* and any deleted (deactivated) classes will appear in the class list. From the list you can use the **Edit** function to make the class active again.

*Once you have transactions entered in the classes, click **Run Reports** to the right of each class found in the **Class List** to bring up a report which includes all the entries for that class to review or print. Use the Back Arrow on your browser to return to the Class List.*

E. LOCATIONS

In addition to **Classes**, QBO offers **Locations.** Locations are designed to be used for separate facilities, i.e., if you have two separate church buildings under one governing group, or a preschool separate from an elementary school. The 40 Classes and Locations limit for the **QuickBooks Plus** subscription is combined, not each.

With locations you can run a full balance sheet as well as a P&L and utilize the classes for the locations as well. Unless you have separate locations, I don't recommend using them in place of classes as you cannot spread expenses from a single transaction across more than one location. For example, when the utility bill comes in, you may want to allocate it to four different departments. If the departments are set up as classes, you can record it to each of them on the bill. But if they are set up as locations, you will have to book it to one location and then make a journal entry for the changes.

F. TAGS

QBO has added an interesting feature called **Tags**. You will see this option on transactions screens like Invoices, Sales Receipts, and Bills. The tags do NOT impact your books, but you can run some reports on them. For example, if your church has a parsonage separate from the church building, you may wish to **Tag** the expenses related to it rather than use a Class. This will only work if the electric, water, and other bills do not need to be spread between more than one tag. But if the parsonage is attached and the electric bill is combined, the tags would not help as you can't separate the expenses.

You could use them to track different small fundraisers or tag people who are responsible for different things. But remember they don't affect the financial statements so you can't make a journal entry to adjust them.

I'm going to show you how to add tags, but I recommend you not worry about these until you are more familiar with the system. They can be a very useful tool, but the reporting and ability to change them are limited, so I'm not going to spend a lot of time on them.

This brings up a screen with some helpful videos you may wish to watch to give you an idea of how to use the tags.

You will notice you have the option to set up a new **Tag group** or **Tag**. If you have a good idea how you will be using the tags, it is a good idea to set up a group first. I'll put in a group called Fundraisers. You can designate a color for that group also.

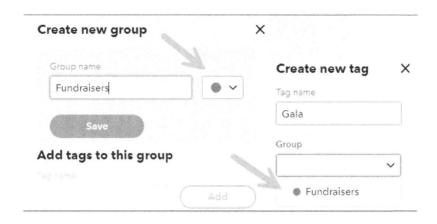

Once the group is set up, go back, and select *New Tag*. Now the screen will have a drop-down menu under **Group** with your group name and color. When you go back to the **Tags** screen, you will see it on the list. Click on the arrow to the left and it will list all the tags under the group. As you tag transactions, the top of the page will have the amounts in **Money In** and **Money Out**.

If you select the **Run Report,** you will see all the transactions that have been marked with that tag. Note at the bottom of the screen you will see the limits allowed for your subscription. For the **Plus** subscription, you are allowed 40 groups and 300 tags.

G. RECORDING THE BEGINNING BALANCE ENTRY

Now that all of your classes have been set up, let's prepare your beginning balance entry. If you will recall, at the end of the last chapter I shared an example beginning balance entry. To record the journal entry, you will need to go to the **+New** (at the top left of your screen) to open a pop-up box with **Customers, Vendors, Employees, and Other.** Select *Other, Journal Entry* in the far-right column

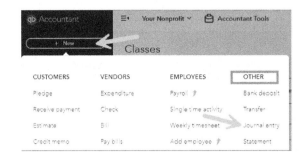

This may bring you to an entry screen. Please note the date will default to today, but you will want to change it to the last da of your previous accounting year. Begin entering the account name for the first line item. The system will "guess" what you want and offer a suggestion. If it is correct, tab over to the next field. If not, use the drop-down menu to find the correct account.

Once you select the correct account name, you will need to enter the amount in either the **Debits** or **Credits** side. For your beginning balance entry, the assets should be *debits* (except accumulated depreciation), and the liabilities and net assets should be *credits*.

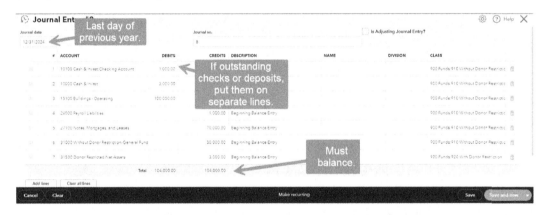

After you have input the dollar amount, tab across to the **Description** field. This is where you explain why you are making the entry. I've put "Beginning Balance Entry" in the example above. Next, skip over the **Name** field—you will very rarely use it. The final column is **Classes.** If you do not see a column for classes, go back to *Gear, Company, Account and Settings, Advanced* and turn on *Track Classes* under **Categories.** In order to compile a correct restricted funds report, every line must have a class. Unless the line item is specifically for a restricted fund, use the **Without Donor Restrictions Fund** class for the balance sheet accounts.

When you enter the account on the next line, QBO will automatically fill in the amount of the opposite side of the entry and the description from the line above. This is because the system requires the entry to be balanced with equal amounts of debits and credits. For multi-line entries like this one, just put the next amount in the correct side, and the system generated amount will be replaced with the correct, balanced amount.

> *Put the **bank statement's ending balance** on one line using the checking account number, and enter **any outstanding deposits** on separate lines with the amounts on the debit side of the entry.*
>
>
> *Any outstanding checks** should be listed separately with the amounts on the credit side of the entry. This will allow you to reconcile your bank account when the previous year's outstanding deposits and checks clear.*

If your organization has specific funds, perhaps named after donors or for specific purposes, you will need to enter each one on a separate line with a class specifically dedicated to it. For each of these net asset accounts, I have chosen a class or sub-class to charge them to. If there were several funds under **Donor Restricted Net Assets**, each would need its own line. Your previous year's auditor or accountant should be able to furnish you with these amounts.

Without Donor Restrictions Net Assets is your general fund balance, but it may not yet equal your audit number. The balance of any accounts receivable and/or accounts payable as of the beginning date is still missing. Remember that you should not enter accounts receivables or accounts payables into this entry. In Chapters 8 and 9, you will input the donors and vendors' open invoices so that this data will be recorded. After your entry balances and you have coded all the net assets to the correct classes, you will press *Save and close.*

Summary

In this chapter we explored how to use classes, including how to:

- Name your classes
- Enter, edit, and delete classes
- Record the beginning balance entry

In the next chapter, we will learn how to set up donors and vendors.

6

DONORS, GRANTS, & PEOPLE
I OWE MONEY TO

A. SETTING UP MEMBERS AND OTHER DONORS

Probably the most important accounting function for organizations is the ability to receive donations and track them to the correct donor. QBO does this by setting up **Donors**. In Chapter 3, we changed the customer label in the Other Preferences from "customer" to "donor" or "member" depending on the main group your organization receives money from.

The process of setting up your donors is easy in QBO. There is even the option to import your donor list from an Excel file. First, I am going to walk you through how to set them up manually in this chapter. This gives you the chance to become familiar with the donor list and trains you in how to add new donors one at a time.

Technically QBO does not have a limit on name lists, but large lists can impact performance. QBO suggests keeping the combined number of names in your company below 10,000. That would include:

- Donors/Members
- Vendors
- Employees
- Products and Services

So, unless you have an exceedingly large donor base, you should have plenty of room. If you are using a donor management system, most of them will have a way to interface with QBO.

1. Adding Donor Types

Before you begin inputting donors, you need to decide how you should organize your donor list. In the business world, this may be wholesale customers or retail customers. If you need data on individual donors' donations versus foundations, you can do this by adding **Donor Types**.

Start by thinking about the types of groups you may need. Do you have Granting Agencies, Foundations, and/or Private Donors? Perhaps you have Members or would like to sort reports by Major Donors, Regular Donors, and Restricted Donors. I recommend looking at any IRS filings or grantee requests to see if there are specific requirements for tracking your donors and working around those.

Once you have determined the Donor Types you want to track, go to the left menu, and select *Sales, Donors*.

The upper right-hand corner has a button called **Donor types.** Click it and a screen will appear with a list of all the current donor types and a green button on the upper right corner called **New donor type.** Select it and a popup box like the one below will appear.

Simply type in the new donor type and *save*. It will add the new donor type to the system and allow you to change the name by selecting *Edit*. The drop-down arrow allows you to **Make inactive.**

2. Adding a New Donor or Member

Are you itching to get those donors' names in the system? Start by selecting *Sales* from the left menu bar, then *Donors*.

This will bring you to a list of donors and their outstanding balances. The down arrow by green **New Donor** button allows you to import donors from other systems or to enter multiple donors at one time.

Let's start by adding a single donor. Select *New donor*. This will bring up the **Donor Information** screen.

The **New Donor** form is quite long and has a lot of information. You won't need to fill out every box but scroll down the form to see what is important to your organization and what isn't. The icons at the top take you down to the different sections of the form.

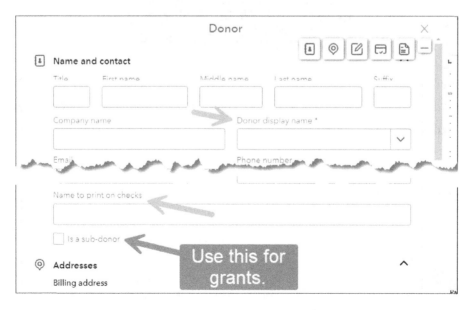

Start at the top of the screen by entering the name of the donor. If the donor is an individual, enter the **First name** and **Last name**. If the donor is an organization or company, enter the **Company name**. **Display name allows** you to determine how the donor's name will be shown on forms and reports.

Email addresses for donors are important as they allow you to easily send receipts and statements from within QBO. Multiple email addresses can be entered to the email field and separated by a comma as long as the total characters in this field do not exceed 100. Enter the multiple email address like this: xxx@gmail.com, yyy@gmail.com.

The **Phone, Mobile, Fax,** and **Website** fields can be entered as needed.

The **Other** field can be used for whatever you would like, but you'll need to keep it consistent across all donors in order to be useful. You may want to use the Other field for a membership number in a club or an envelope number in a church. Play around and see what use of this field fits your needs the best.

For now, I will skip the sub-donor part and will explain in detail how to use this feature in the next section. The next section is Addresses. Enter up to two addresses, billing, and shipping, for each donor.

Notes and attachments is a handy place to write information about the donor you might want to have handy, i.e., the donor is related to a teacher in the school or is on a particular committee. QBO allows you to have a maximum of 4,000 characters in the Customer Notes field. If you click on *Add attachments* a list of your computer files will appear to select from. You can also highlight a file from your desktop or other computer area and carry it to this place. Use this feature to store any documentation regarding the invoice (a scanned pledge card, perhaps) or to upload grant documents, letters, baptismal or wedding documents, etc.

Payments allow you to set defaults for that donor on the invoice or sales receipt screens. If you send out pledge reminders or have some type of membership dues, you may wish to use the **Terms** field. This is less important in a nonprofit than a business. The drop-down arrow offers several payment term options, or you can add your own. **Preferred delivery method** allows you to send out statements via email or print.

The **Additional info** is where you will designate the **Donor type** and note tax exemptions. Most of you will probably not charge sales tax, but if you sell goods through your organization, it may come in handy. As every state has different regulations, you need to check with your accountant to be sure.

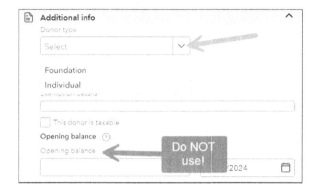

The **Opening balance** needs to be ignored. If the donor owes the organization money, it must be entered as a receivable, which I'll show you how to record in Chapter 8.

The **Additional Info** tab allows you to link the donor to one of the Donor Types we set up earlier.

3. Grouping Donors: Parent and Sub-Donors

Earlier I showed you a small box on the Donor Information form titled **Is sub-donor.** You may want to use sub-donors if you have a grantee organization that has given you more than one grant to track. In this case, you will set up the organization as the **Parent donor,** and each of the grants as **Sub-donors.**

To create a parent group, you will first create a new donor as we learned above.

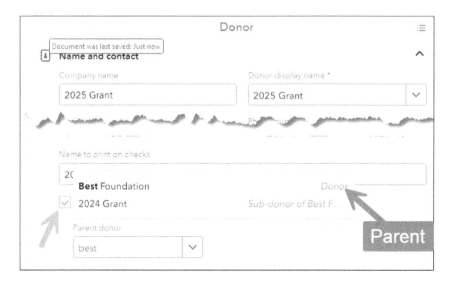

In this example, we are creating a donor called "Best Foundations." Next, we will set up donors for each of the grants. While doing this, click **Is a sub-donor** box. You can select Best Foundations from the parent donor drop-down menu or start typing the name to bring it up. Finally, depending on the grant agreement, choose either **Bill this donor** or **Bill with parent**. Click *Save*.

For this example, I have two donors to be sub-donors of this group, so my donor list looks like this:

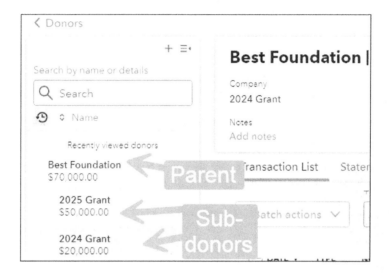

Note the total of the sub-donor amounts equals the parent amount.

4. **Batch Actions on the Donor Contact List**

You can select some of your donors to make inactive, email, or change the donor type by clicking on the left side of the donors' names that you want to change.

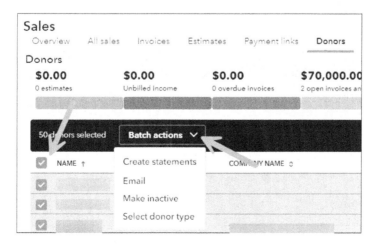

To change all of the donors, select the box next to **NAME** at the top. Then follow the prompts for the action requested.

B. VIEWING & PRINTING THE DONOR CONTACT LIST REPORT

The donor/member list is a very important tool to any non-profit organization or church. Many times, donor information needs to be shared with leadership for planning purposes. The report can also be helpful as you figure out how to organize your donor list. In Chapter 12, we will go into detail about reports, but let's take a moment to learn how to view the **Donor Contact List** you have created.

Select *Reports* from the left menu bar. Next, choose the *Standard* tab. Scroll down to the **Sales and customers** box and click on *Donor Contact List*. You can also type the report name in the search box. If you click on the Star icon, it will save the report in a Favorites area at the top of the report list.

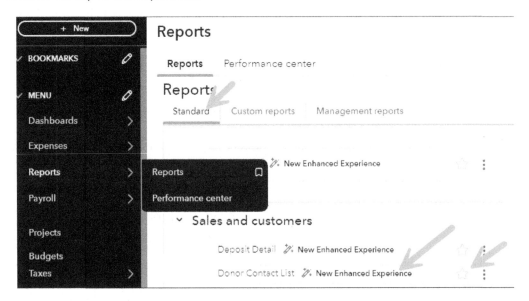

This brings you to the **Donor Contact List** which contains all of the Donors you have entered thus far in QBO.

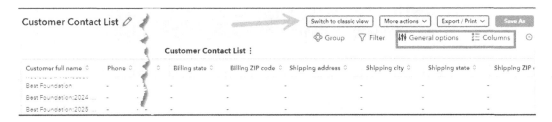

Review it in detail. I find it helpful to visit this list while entering donors to make sure that each is categorized correctly, paying special attention to the appropriate parent grouping. Review the list and double click on any name to **Edit** function. You can email, print, or export it to Excel or PDF by **Export/Print** box in the upper right corner.

You can customize the report with the **General options** and **Columns**. I'll explain additional customization options for all reports in a later chapter. Great job! Now let's set up vendors.

C. SETTING UP VENDORS (THE PEOPLE YOU PAY)

If you select *Expenses*, *Vendors* from the left menu bar, you will see a screen in the same format as the Customer/Donor screen. To add a new vendor, select *New vendor* from the top of the list.

If the vendor is an individual, enter the **First name** and **Last name**. If the vendor is an organization or company, enter the **Company**. Just like the donor entry screen, you will then choose how the donor's name is displayed on forms and reports.

If you need to cut separate checks to the same company (perhaps different insurance plans), you will want to have different Vendor Names. *123 Insurance-Building* and *123 Insurance-Liability* are possible examples. Like the new donor screen, you can change the titles of any of the boxes with drop-down arrows.

The **Name to print on checks** is handy when the company name is different than whom they would like the check made out to. If you leave it blank, it will take the Company name from above.

Similar to the **Donor Information** screen, multiple email addresses can be entered to the **Email** field and separated by a comma as long as the total characters in this field do not exceed 100. Multiple email addresses are entered as follows: xxx@gmail.com, yyy@gmail.com.

Notes and attachments are like the donors' area. Here is a great place to upload a scan of your independent contractors' W-9.

ACH payments have an area for your vendor's bank account and routing numbers so you can pay them without a check through QuickBooks Payments system. This is a huge time saver as you don't have to print and mail checks and the system automatically marks the bills as paid.

Additional info is where you will designate someone as an independent contractor. There is a place for their business EIN or SSN. Click the box next to **Track payments for 1099** for individuals you will need to send 1099 to. This will bring up the vendor's information at year end, so you can make the final determination. For detailed information on how to know if a vendor is an independent contractor, please read either of my books, *Nonprofit Accounting for Volunteers, Treasurers, & Bookkeepers or Church Accounting-The How-To Guide for Small & Growing Churches.*

You probably don't need to worry about the **Billing rate** unless you use it for grant invoices. **Payments** is where you can input any terms and account numbers you have with vendors.

Under **Accounting**, use the dropdown arrow to pick the expense account most often used with this vendor. When you open a bill and put in the vendor's name, the form will populate with this account number to save you time.

Do NOT use the opening balance. I'll show you how to enter open invoices in chapter 10. **Account no** is the vendor's accountant number that is displayed on their bills. It will be printed on the memo line of checks to that vendor.

 Do Not Use the Opening Balance!! You will take care of that in Chapter 9.

The **Business ID** is where you will store the Employer Identification Number (EIN), or Social Security number for any non-corporate vendors you expect to spend more than $600 a year with.

D. IMPORTING DONOR AND VENDOR LIST FROM A SPREADSHEET

You may enter the donor or member data by uploading a Microsoft Excel spreadsheet (Excel must already be on your computer) or by copying and pasting it into the **Multiple donors** page. To **Import** donors, select *Sales, Donors* from the **Left Menu**. Go to the drop-down arrow to the right of the **New donor** button. Click *Import donors.*

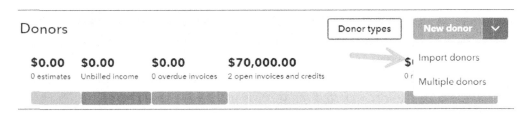

On the **Import Donors** screen, select *Download a sample file* located just below the upload field.

Save the sample Microsoft Excel file to the desktop or other easily found location. It will become the template for your donor or member data.

Use the sample data provided as a guide, but you can leave fields blank that do not apply or you don't currently have the information for. Part of the reason I had you set up a donor manually was so you could see which fields you wanted to use, and which are okay to leave blank (i.e., leave the company field blank if the donor is an individual).

Each column in your worksheet should be in the same cell format as the example file, i.e., if the date shows year-month-day, key in 20xx-xx-xx, not xx/xx/xx. Enter your donor or member information in the appropriate fields as listed.

If your spreadsheet was downloaded from your contact base with the columns in a different order, move them to mirror the columns in the example file, i.e. A=Name, B=Company, C=Customer Type, etc. Remember that all of the columns do not have to be filled in. Some donors may not have email addresses, a website, or fax numbers for example. You may also delete columns that are not needed for your donors.

 *Do **NOT** include the Opening Balance column. These amounts will be input later as invoices.*

Unfortunately, you cannot make sub-donors during this process. You will have to go back to the individual donor records and select the Parent after the donors are uploaded.

 The more complete you can make the information in the spreadsheet before it is imported, the less you will have to do later.

Once all the data is complete in your spreadsheet, save it to your desktop or other easily found location. **Don't forget to delete all of the sample donor information from the template before proceeding.**

To import the file, from the **Main menu,** select *Sales, Donors,* click on the drop-down arrow beside **New donor** and *Import donors.* Click on the **Browse** button and locate the donor file you have updated and saved. Click *Next.*

Now it is time to **Map your fields to QuickBooks fields.** This process will point the fields from your spreadsheet to the corresponding field in QBO. The system pulls the column names from your spreadsheet and tries to line it up to the **QUICKBOOKS ONLINE FIELD.**

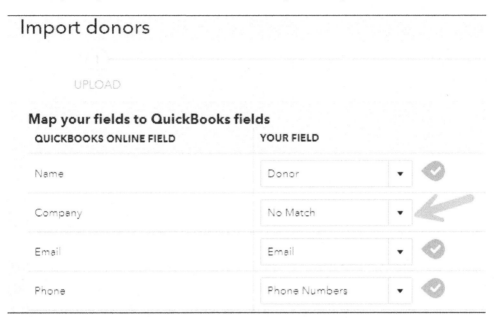

Review each field. A green icon with a check will tell you QBO has matched the field to theirs. For the items without a match, use the arrow to see if you can find one. If not, hit the *Back* button on the lower left side of the screen to take you back to the import page. Pull up your spreadsheet, make the necessary changes and try again.

If you used the Microsoft Excel template provided, you will probably not have many changes to make. After you have made any necessary corrections, select *Next* to import the data. You will receive a success message indicating the number of records that have been imported.

1. **Multiple donors**

You may find it easier to copy individual columns from a spreadsheet into a **Batch transactions** screen. To access go to the **Left Menu,** *Sales, Donors,* down arrow next to **New donor**, *Multiple donors.*

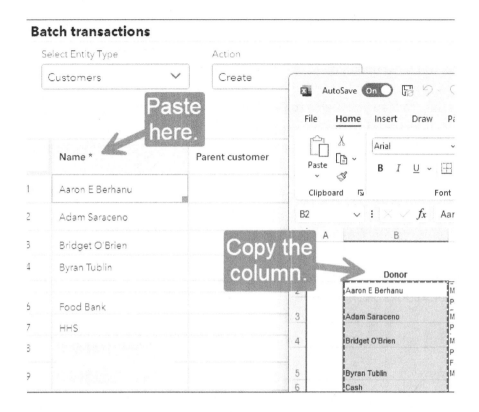

A screen with headers matching QuickBooks fields will show up. You may then copy the data from a single column of a spreadsheet and then paste it under the proper heading. This approach will also let you assign the parent customer using the drop-down arrows.

Once you are happy with the columns, click *Save*. The system will tell you how many imported and any who didn't will show back up on the screen to you to change.

The examples we just completed were for donors. Repeat the same process for your vendors by going back to the **Main Menu** and selecting *Expenses, Vendors, Import vendors or Multiple vendors.*

E. PROJECTS

As I mentioned earlier, QBO allows you to track grants via sub-donors or through **Projects**. If it is a simple grant that you simply need to track basic expenses to, the sub-donor function is sufficient. But if you need to track employee hours worked on the grant and give detailed "in process" reports, I recommend you use the Projects feature.

Turn on Projects by going to *Gear, Your Company, Account and Settings, Advanced.*

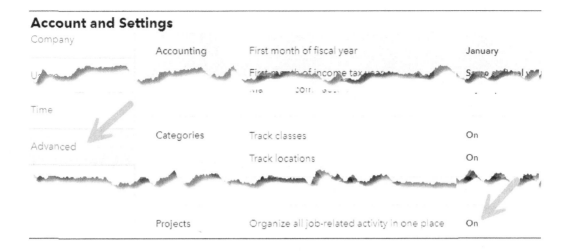

Account and Settings

To access **Projects**, go to the **Left Menu** and select *Projects*. An introductory screen will appear. Select *Start a project*.

Under **Project name** give the grant the name the people in your organization will understand but do **NOT** use the same name as a sub-donor. Trust me, it will be very confusing for you on the transaction entry screens if you do.

Use the drop-down arrow under **Donor** to select from your donor list. Under **Notes** be sure to put in the basic information on the grant to make it easy for you to identify later. **Save** the project.

Your Projects home screen will now list this grant and any others you may add.

If you aren't sure if you should track your grants by sub-donor or by project, start with the sub-donor. The system will let you convert the sub-donor to a project on this screen if you need the additional capabilities.

Once you have multiple projects, you can sort them by status and customer/donor or use the Search box. Use **New project** to add more grants or projects. The screen will show the projects, income received and related costs, the profit margin, and time spent. Under the **Actions** area, select *Options* to edit, cancel, show it complete or delete the project.

At the top is a button titled **Hourly cost rate**. Select it if your employees track their time by project, you can use this to develop an accurate cost per hour. After you have set up Employees in the **Workers** menu, the list will populate with all your employees. The **COST RATE** will be blank. Click on the *calculator* icon to see a pop-up that allows you to determine your hourly cost.

Employee hourly rate

Include the total of wages, taxes, and overhead for each worker. *This is not your billable rate.*

EMPLOYEE	COST RATE
Lisa London e	

Hourly cost rate calculator

Wages (/hr)	
Employer taxes (/hr) (7.65% - Social Security & Medicare)	
Additional employer taxes (/hr) (SUTA, FUTA, etc.)	
Workers' compensation (/hr)	
Overhead (/hr)	
Total hourly cost rate	$0.00

Cancel   Add

Please note-this is NOT your billable rate. It is the actual cost to your organization of this employee. If you are using the QBO payroll feature, the calculator will automatically populate with your employees' **Wages per hour** and the **Employer taxes per hour**. If not, when you enter the hourly rate manually, the employer tax is calculated.

The next three boxes allow you to add additional amounts for unemployment taxes, worker compensation, or an overhead rate. The overhead rate would include health benefits, paid leave, etc. You can calculate the cost per hour by adding up the annual costs of these for the employee and dividing it by the number of hours he is expected to work in a year.

Once you are happy with the numbers, select *Add* and continue to the next employee.

You will add the income and the expenses to this project as you receive money and pay bills, which we will go over in future chapters.

Summary

In this chapter, you have learned how to handle donor accounts, including how to:

- Set up members and other donors
- Determine donor type
- Add a new donor or member
- Group donors: parent and sub-donors
- View & print the donor contact list report
- Set up vendors (the people you pay)
- Import donor and vendor lists from a spreadsheet
- Set up a project to track a grant

Once you have added your donor and vendor lists, you are almost ready to input transactions, like donations and checks. In the next chapter, I'll first explain how **Products and Services (Items)** are used to facilitate the process.

Z

PRODUCTS & SERVICES
—TRACKING THE TRANSACTIONS

Recall in the first chapter how I explained the importance of lists. One of these lists is **Products and Services**. QuickBooks Online uses **Products and Services** to track revenues and expenditures. If you have used the desktop version of QuickBooks, you know them as **Items**. The term "Items" is used in QBO when entering expense transactions, so I will use these terms interchangeably.

By using products and services (items), QBO does the accounting for normal recurring transactions without requiring you to remember the account numbers. In a business, the items would be the goods or services available to sell or to purchase. For a nonprofit or church, the items will be donations, grants, membership dues, designated programs, tithes, offerings, capital campaigns, etc. This is how you will track the money coming in. You may also set up items for recurring purchases or for tracking volunteer hours.

A. PRODUCT AND SERVICE TYPES

There are three different product and service types.

Non-inventory parts—use this for items you sell but don't need to inventory, i.e., magazine subscriptions.

Service—most of your receipts, including your donations, grants, tithes, and funds collected for other organizations, will be the Service type.

Bundle—A collection of products and/or services that you sell together.

Inventory part—if you sell tee shirts, books, or other things that you buy to resell, and need to keep track of the amount on hand, you will use this.

If you are familiar with the desktop version of QuickBooks, please note the products and services types listed above are used to record the following:

- **Other charges**—used for fines or service charges. You probably won't use this much.
- **Group**—I'll show you how to use this for allocations.
- **Payments**—record the payment received when you prepare the invoice.
- **Sales tax item and Sales tax group**—if you are selling goods that your state requires you to collect sales taxes on, you will need a sales tax item.

B. SETTING UP NEW PRODUCTS AND SERVICES

I'll start with the **Service** type. Your most important service is probably **Donations.** Like the Chart of Accounts, Products and Services can have sub-items. For your **Donation** item, you can establish sub-items such as **Dues, Plate Offerings, Online Giving,** and **Donations.** Don't worry about entering all possibilities. It is easy to add more products and services as you need them.

 There should be an item set up for every revenue line item on your chart of accounts. If you would like to track additional detail, use Sub-products/ services.

Let's set up a service item. There are two ways to access the **Product and Services**. From the gear menu under *List*, select **Products and Services** or go to the **Left Menu,** *Sales, Products & Services.*

After arriving at the **Products and Services** list, select *New.*

You will start by selecting the **Type** of item. Our example will be a service item. Assign the item a **Name.** The **SKU** (Item number if you are familiar with the desktop version) is rarely necessary. Just like donors, products/services can have a parent and a sub-item. If it is a **Sub-product/service**, select *Is sub-product/service* and associate it with a parent service using the drop-down arrow, like you did in in Chapter 6 with sub-donors.

Next is **Class.** Always assign a class to a new item and it will save you tons of reclassing time later. Any information you key into the **Description** box will display on invoices (donation form), so be sure your spelling is correct, and the description would make sense to the donor. This can be overridden when you enter the transaction.

Products and services allow you to designate a flat **Sales price/rate**, say $100 honorarium to speak at a function. If the item you are entering has a standard rate, input it here; otherwise leave it blank. The invoice screens will allow you to override this amount. Any parent item should have a rate of $0. The revenue recorded for a transaction with this item will go into the **Income account** you designate. The drop-down menu allows you to select from the chart of accounts.

Once you are happy with the description, amount, and the account the product will go to, select **Save and close** to exit the **Product/Service information** screen or click on the drop-down arrow to select *Save and new* to continue entering other items.

You will notice a redundancy in the items and the chart of accounts. If you do not need your financial statements to list the different types of donations, you can set up one donation account with lots of items that record into it. Read Chapter 12 on Reports and ask your Board of Directors what level of detail they would like to see.

Before we move onto the next chapter, I would like to summarize the difference between using classes and adding new accounts or items.

Classes	Admin				Education				Outreach			
Account	Donation		Utilities		Donation		Utilities		Donation		Utilities	
Item	Pledges	Unpledged support	Water	Electric	Pledges	Unpledged support	Water	Electric	Pledges	Unpledged support	Water	Electric

In my example above, the organization has three programs: Admin, Education and Outreach. Because each will have revenues (donations) and expenses, we need to track them via **Classes**. The revenues and expenses are shown on the financial statements as **Accounts**. Because we want more detail available that we don't need to show on the financial statements, we use **Items (Products/Services)** to track Pledged and Unpledged support and Water and Electricity.

Product/Services/Items are used to identify the specific things you receive donations for or to track very specific expenses. They are used to bill your donors and to allocate expenses to programs and grants. For example, you may have items set up for three different types of donations which feed into one Donations account. Likewise, your Utility account may have Water, Electric, and Gas items. Reports can be run to show all costs to specific items.

Account numbers are used to track revenues, expenditures, assets, and liabilities to show on your financial statements. Each item is linked to an account number, but each account may have more than one item.

There will be quite a bit of redundancy between the account numbers and the items. You can limit the number of accounts by putting the details in Items. If you need to see how much you spent on electricity, a report on the Item *Electricity* can be run without having to have a separate account on the financial statements.

Classes can be used as separate general ledgers to track the money received and spent for a particular program or fund. Account numbers are assigned classes when a transaction is recorded, so the amounts can be compiled together as individualized financial statements for each of the programs and funds.

Summary

In this chapter you learned

- What Product/Services are and how they are used
- The different type of Products/Services
- How to add them
- When to use Products/Services vs Classes vs Accounts

In the next chapter, you will learn how to handle money received.

8

MONEY IN
—RECORDING DONATIONS & REVENUES

In order for your organization or church to continue to do its good work, money needs to come in the door. As responsible stewards of your donors' donations, you must implement accounting procedures and systems that will allow you to record and track the dollars while keeping the money safe. Before you learn how to enter the money received, I'll walk you through some basic internal accounting controls.

A. ACCOUNTING CONTROLS FOR RECEIPTS

If you keep in mind two basic guidelines, most of the controls I recommend will make sense.

First, **no one should have access to cash and checks without other people observing them**.

Second, **if a person has access to the accounting system (in this case, QBO), he should not have access to the money-this includes any online donation programs**.

This means the treasurer should be a different person than the bookkeeper, or if that is not possible, the treasurer should not have access to the bank account. Most thefts happen when the person handling the money can adjust the books to hide their actions. I highly recommend going back to Chapter 1 to reread the **Case for Internal Accounting Controls** and **Points for the Board.**

 Don't start shaking your head and saying, "But we are too small to have those kinds of controls." No organization is too small to protect both their volunteers and employees from suspicion and ensure their funds from mismanagement.

In order to design controls for your organization or church, think about the way the money is received. Membership fees are paid via cash or check at meetings; a collection basket is passed around during the service; checks are received in the mail; electronic payments are made through the website; etc. Take time to walk through any scenario in which you receive money and design procedures that will not conflict with the two guidelines above. Here are some basic steps for the most common ways of receiving money.

B. MONEY RECEIVED DURING MEETINGS OR FUNDRAISERS

If your organization is large enough to have a physical location and staff, it is much easier to design basic controls over the money coming in. But even if most of the money comes in during club meetings or fundraisers, controls can still be utilized.

 Basic requirements when the person recording the books is also the person collecting the money:

- The bookkeeper is not a check signer or has access to online banking or credit card programs.
- The person collecting the money must stay in plain sight during the meeting or event where money is collected.
- A receipt book with self-duplicating pages must be utilized. If a member pays for something with cash, he should receive a paper receipt. The organization then has copies of these receipts in chronological order.
- At the end of the meeting or event, two people should total the checks and cash together and compare the monies received with the receipt book. They then sign a summary sheet of paper with their names and the date.

C. MONEY RECEIVED DURING RELIGIOUS SERVICES

Most churches will pass the plate or a basket for offerings or donations during their weekly services. This money is often brought to the front of the sanctuary for the remainder of the service or is taken to another secured area of the church. If it is taken to the front of the sanctuary in full view of the congregation, it will need to be collected after the service by two people. These are usually people that will also be the "counters," i.e., they will count the money and record on a piece of paper or deposit slip how much was received.

Whether at the front of the church or in a separate room, until the dollar amount of money is recorded, the collection should be seen by at least two people. I also recommend not allowing married couples or people living in the same household to be counters together as there is more likelihood of collusion.

I like to have the members of the governing board rotate as counters with the other volunteers. It allows the board members to keep an eye on the day-to-day workings of the church.

The counters, neither of which should be the bookkeeper, will count the cash and make copies of the checks or record each of them manually. The counters fill out a summary form and sign it. The total on the form must match the bank deposit. The deposit will then be driven to the bank and put in the night deposit. One person can do this as there is a record of the receipts at the church. When the bookkeeper comes to work later that week, he or she will have a copy of the summary form to record each donor's or member's offering.

If an offering envelope system is used to track contributions, the counters must:

- Verify the money in the envelope matches the amount stated on the envelope and note it as cash or check.
- Bring discrepancies to the team leader's attention before correcting the envelope.
- If a check, make sure the check number is included on the envelope.
- Complete blank envelopes with check information if check is enclosed.
- Include any cash received in blank envelopes in the loose offering total.
- Batch and total envelopes and deliver to bookkeeper for entry.

D. MONEY RECEIVED THROUGH THE MAIL

Nonprofits often receive their donations through the mail; therefore, it is a good idea to have a post office box. This keeps anyone from stealing the checks directly out of your mailbox. However, you don't want your bookkeeper to be the one to pick up the mail. Theoretically, he could steal a check, but adjust the donor's account to look like it was received.

Designate someone without access to the accounting system to go to the post office, and then, back at the organization, have him open the mail in front of a second person.

Each check should then be recorded, and the summary signed by the two observers. If you have an RID scanner, scan the checks immediately, and then give the deposit report and the marked checks to the bookkeeper.

E. PAYMENTS RECEIVED THROUGH THE WEBSITE OR MOBILE SITES

Now that so much is being done on the web, many organizations have found it advantageous to add a donation button to their website via PayPal® or any of many other services. It is crucial that you safeguard the link to the bank account. Many online credit card processors will require signed corporate resolutions stating you are a legal organization and the check signers have authorized the funds to go to that account. Others, like PayPal, simply use an email/password combination. This is potentially problematic as the person who has the password could reroute the appointed deposit bank account to their personal account number.

 A PayPal employee told me of a women associated with a small nonprofit who had set up its PayPal account. She had a falling out with the organization and refused to tell them the password to collect the money.

To keep this from occurring with your organization, I would recommend the account be linked to an email address administered by your organization (admin@yourorganization.org) and assigned to someone who has no access to the donors' records. This person would have the authorization to change the bank deposit account and permit transfers from the PayPal account to the bank.

PayPal allows for a secondary user with limited rights. The secondary user can only see reports, not change bank accounts. You will want this to be your bookkeeper so he can reconcile the receipts in PayPal to the cash posted into the bank. Any discrepancies should be investigated immediately.

Any software or website you are using to collect money needs to be analyzed to assure no unauthorized persons can change the bank account the credit card swipes or transfers go to. If you are unsure, contact the developer and ask.

We've covered some basic steps to protect your people and your money in the most common ways donations are received. Now make a list of all the ways your organization receives money and, for each case, ask yourself, "How can I get it to the bank and recorded in the financial statements while safeguarding the funds and my volunteers and employees?"

These are the minimum steps necessary to safeguard receipts. If your organization already has more complete procedures, please follow them.

F. ENTERING DONATIONS

1. Entering Simple Donations

The money you receive may be simple donations. By simple, I mean that the donor does not expect to be invoiced or given a receipt at the time of the donation. This is also the easiest way to enter receipts into QBO.

Go to + *New, Donors, Sales Receipt* to reach the Sales Receipt screen.

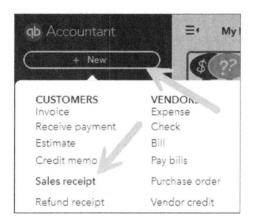

You may also access Sales Receipts through *Menu, Sales, All sales, New transaction, Sales Receipt.*

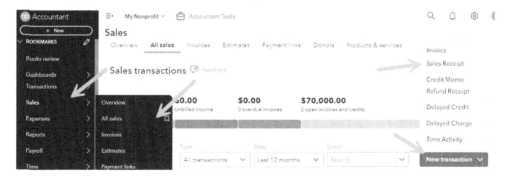

This is where all of the work you've done in setting up your lists pays off. The chart of accounts, donors/members, products/services (items), and class lists are all used to tell QBO what the source and purpose of the money coming is and where you will put it. Let's take a look at the sales receipt.

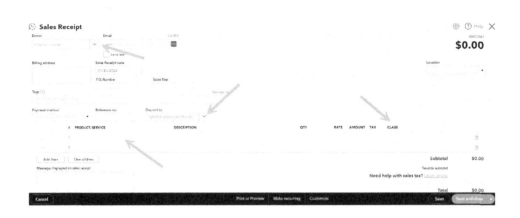

A sales receipt is required for each separate donor included in that day's deposit. It is important that the person opening the mail or taking payments is documenting all of these details, so the bookkeeper is able to enter data in these fields. Sales receipts will also be used if you are bringing money in from online donations.

There is a lot of information on this screen. In the box marked **Donor**, begin typing the donor's name (or code, if you didn't use last names), and the system will pull up donor names. In this example, I had only typed an "best," and the system brought up all the names that started with best in them, including sub-donors. If you are using sub-donors, be sure you select the correct one.

 If you have receipts that do not need to be tracked by donor, enter them into QBO by setting up a "Miscellaneous" donor and then enter the donations on separate lines for each donation type.

The system will fill in the email, billing, and shipping addresses automatically. You may select **Add New** if the donor is not already listed. The **Sales Receipt date** is when the funds were received by your organization, not necessarily when you recorded them.

Location is the option you may have set up in **Gear, Your Company, Account and Settings, Advanced, Categories, Locations,** if you wanted to track locations.

PO Number and **Sales Rep** can be used for donation identifiers and responsible employees but are not required. **Tags**, as I explained in Chapter 5, are optional and new ones are easily added in this screen.

Select the appropriate **Payment method** (check, cash, credit card, etc.) from the drop-down menu and enter the check number if applicable. If the donor gave both cash and check in the same donation, you would need to enter it as two separate donations. Only one payment method can be selected for each receipt.

When entering the data, pay close attention to the **Deposit to** account. This should be *Undeposited Funds* as the **Deposit to** account. I'll explain this in much greater detail a little later in this chapter, but for now, think of **Undeposited Funds** as the virtual stack of checks and money you have in a bank bag. The actual checks and cash may already have been deposited, but making this selection ensures this deposit will be batched properly in QBO. You will thank me later when it's time to reconcile the bank account, which I will tell you about in Chapter 11.

The **Product Service** will be Donations or similar item you had previously set up or can add at this screen via the drop-down arrow. The **Description** will automatically fill from the Product Service, but you can override it. If you had established a rate when you set up the service, QBO will automatically enter it.

> *The first time you enter a donation in the sales receipt screen, you may feel a little confused with using items (I know I did). Just remember that items are simply the details that feed into the reports.*

Back in Chapter 7, you set up the types of donations and other receipts in items. Now you will use them on the sales receipt.

Then, designate a class based on the program the donation is supporting, or use the unrestricted fund class.

Always enter a **Class**! It may be chosen from the drop-down menu or may fill automatically if the donor was set up that way. You can type a message in the box that will show up on the receipt if you are printing or emailing it to the donor. Below that box is an area to insert **Attachments.**

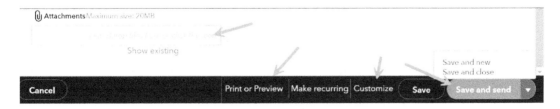

At the bottom is a **Make recurring** and a **Customize option**. I'll be showing you how those work later in the book.

Select *Save & new* from the drop-down arrow at the bottom, and a blank sales receipt or donation screen appears ready for you to add the next donation. **Save** will save the receipt but keep you in the screen, **Save and close** will take you back to the previous screen you were on. **Save and send** will send an email to the donor.

G. ACKNOWLEDGING THE DONATION

After entering the donation, you may print or email it. The donation acknowledgement can be printed or sent as you are entering each one, or you can print/send them as a batch after you finish entering that day's receipts.

QBO has a convenient feature which allows you to customize the acknowledgement emailed to your donor. This is very handy as the IRS requires specific wording for acknowledgements to donors for gifts over $250. I'll go over the customization process in Chapter 15.

If you are emailing one donor at a time, you will send the email before you leave the donor receipt screen. At the bottom right corner, click the down arrow and select *Save and send*.

The next window allows you to edit the individual donor's message on the email screen before you send it.

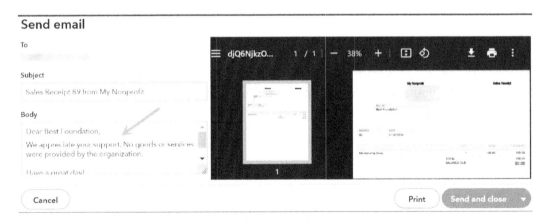

Type in your personalized message. Click *Save and send* to email the donor. If you want to send all the sales receipt emails at once, check the *Send later* block located just below the donor email address on the sales receipt.

For a receipt to be included in a batch, the **Send later** box must be checked for that sales receipt. The donor email address will populate automatically if you had included it during the donor set up in Chapter 6, or you can enter it here.

If you prefer to print the sales receipts, deselect the **Send later** box and go to the bottom of the sales entry screen. Click *Print or Preview*, and check *Print later*.

When you are ready to send or print, from the left **Menu,** select *Sales, All Sales*. You will then arrive at the **Sales Transactions** screen.

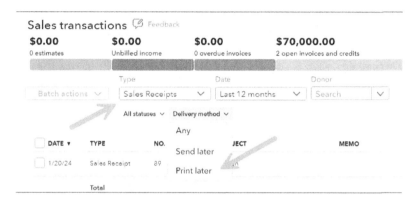

You can filter what you will see by selecting the drop-down arrow under **Type**, select *Sales Receipts*; under **Status,** choose *All statuses*; and for the **Delivery method,** select *Print later* or *Send later*. Click *Apply*. Your donation acknowledgements you had held are now automatically sent to your donors or printed for you to mail.

I'll discuss how to customize forms and reports in Chapter 15 so your donors or members can learn about the great work you are doing.

H. ENTERING CASH RECEIPTS

Let's set up a donor called **Cash** for cash donations or "loose plate" offerings that are not attributed to a specific donor.

You can add new donors directly from the **Sales Receipt** screen *(+New, Sales Receipts)* without having to go back to the donor list. Select the **Choose a donor** drop-down menu and then select *Add new*.

Now make the **New Donor Name** *Cash.* You do not need to input any details. Click *Save.* The **Sales Receipt** screen will appear with **Cash** in the donor field.

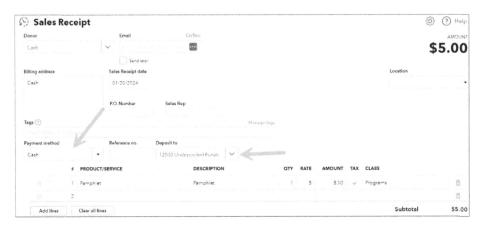

In this example, an informational pamphlet was sold. Select the appropriate **Class**, set the **Payment method** to *Cash,* and the **Item** to *Publications.* Input the amount (it can go under **Rate** or **Amount**) and *Save and close.* If you are using the **Location** option, you'll also need to enter it.

I. ENTERING DONATIONS FROM A SEPARATE DONOR BASE

You do not have to track your donors through QBO. Many nonprofits and churches use internet-based donor record systems. These databases offer more flexibility in analysis and in correspondence with the donors. If you are looking for a new donor database management system, I recommend looking at those that automatically flow into QBO. It will save you tons of time.

Some offer an app or download option to easily import the data into QBO. Others will require you to make a manual entry. Without knowing which database you are using, I can't walk you through that step, but the database company will have instructions for you. I can, however, show you how to enter it manually. Start by setting up a new donor called Donor Database. Run a report from your donor database system that totals the donations for the day, week, or month you will be entering.

Be sure to group the donations from the database to match the deposits made in the bank. For example, if you received 10 donations throughout the week and went to the bank to deposit them two different times, you will need the report to list the donations based on each day deposited.

Bring up the **Sales Receipt (Donation)** screen.

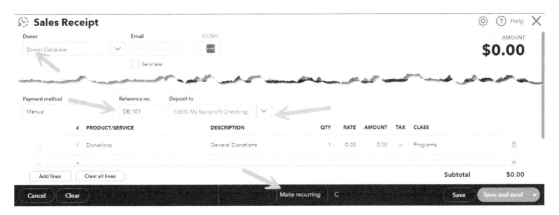

Select the customer **Donor Database** and choose the correct class (unrestricted for regular donations, or specific program class). Input the day these donations were deposited in the **Sales Receipt Date** box.

The **Reference No.** should be the report reference number from the donor system. You will not need to input a check number or payment method. Designate the items and amount of the first daily deposits from the donor database report and then select *Save & new*. Continue entering the amounts of the next deposit date from the report.

You can set this up as a **Recurring Receipt** by selecting *Make recurring*. I'll show you how to do this later in the chapter. Just remember that if you do it this way, you'll need to edit the future receipts for the correct amounts that week or month.

J. DUES & PLEDGES—BILLING AND PAYMENT

1. Recording Dues or Pledges as Receivables

If your organization asks its donors or members to pay dues annually or for a project, QBO can track them. If you are a religious organization with members who tithe or pledge, QBO can also help. The system uses **Invoices** to bill for **Dues or Pledges** from **Donors or Members**. Go to *+New, Invoice* (found under **CUSTOMERS)** or *Menu, Sales, Invoice, Create Invoice*. The **Invoice** screen will appear.

You will notice this looks like the **Sales Receipt** screen. Be careful to pay attention that you are on the correct entry screen. The names of the screen are always in the top left of the heading.

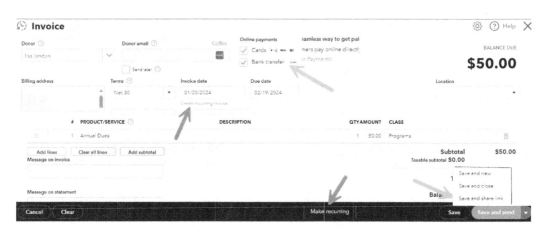

Enter the donor's name, today's date, due date, amount and select the appropriate Product/Service; in this case, **Annual Dues**. If you haven't already set up Annual Dues, simply type in the name and select the **Add new** option. The new Product/Services screen will appear and let you add it right there.

The system will fill in the predesignated amount from the Product/Service entered. At the top of the screen is the **Online Payment** option. Intuit, the company that makes QBO, has credit card processing and bank transfer services you can sign up for. There is a fee, but it is very competitive with other processors and has the benefit of recording the transaction, so you don't have to. If possible, I strongly recommend using QuickBooks Payments.

If you have signed up for this service, select both the Cards and Bank transfer options. When you email the invoice to the donor or member, he will be able to click directly on the email and pay the bill. The system will automatically record the payment.

To save, you have the option *to Save and close, Save and new,* and *Save and share link.* The **Share Link** option is a great way to add a link to this invoice and payment request to an email you are writing outside the system.

Once you select *Save & new,* you will be directed back to the empty invoice screen. Continue entering dues and close. If you are entering dues received for the following year, date the dues on January 1 of the next year, otherwise keep today's date. The email and print options are the same as described earlier in this chapter in the section titled **Acknowledging the Donation**.

2. **Recording Monthly/Recurring Dues or Pledge Installments**

If your members or donors make payments to you on a recurring basis (monthly, quarterly, etc.), you can enter the first period amount and have the system record the future charges using the **Make recurring** option.

After entering the dues amount, check to make sure your invoice has the exact items (products/services) and amount you want to bill each period. Then select **Make recurring** at the bottom of the invoice entry screen or under the **Invoice Date** box. The recurring transaction will be exactly what was in your invoice.

You will arrive at the **Recurring Invoice** screen that has several options. The **Type** field allows you to choose to have QBO remind you to record the entry manually (**Reminder**) or automatically record it (**Scheduled**). **Scheduled** transactions will automatically be posted to QBO. You would only do this for transactions that retain the amount, category account and class for each period. **Unscheduled** and **Reminder templates** can be pulled up and edited before they are used as needed from the Recurring Transactions list.

Choose how many **Days in Advance to Enter** into the register. I'd use seven days in advance, so you know it is coming. **Unscheduled** adds the template to the Recurring Transaction list so you can access it as needed.

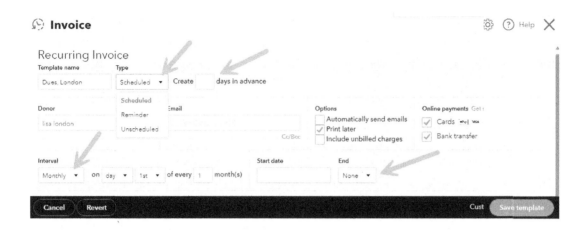

Select the **Interval** it should be recorded, the **Start date**, the **End date,** and. You can also select to **Automatically send emails** to the donor.

Always put a number in the **End date** or it will keep posting for eternity. I like to have them stop at the end of the fiscal year and then reset them for the new year. *Select* **Save template**.

3. **Manage Recurring Transactions**

All **Recurring Transactions** are stored in a list by the same name. Go to *Gear icon, Lists, Recurring Transactions.*

The list of **Recurring Transactions** allows you to add **New** transactions from this screen. The list shows the templates, their type (Scheduled, Reminder, or Unscheduled) and the intervals.

Click the downward arrow to the right of the **Edit** option to access the **Use, Duplicate, Pause, Skip next date,** and **Delete** options.

K. ENTERING BEGINNING RECEIVABLE BALANCES

If your organization had open receivables as of the start date, you would need to enter them as invoices dated in the previous accounting year. For example, assume you had three donors with outstanding dues of $1000 each as of December 31, 2023, and you are setting up QBO with a start date of January 1, 2024. For each donor, enter an invoice dated in 2023 for $1000. This will make your beginning balances as of January 1 correct and will give you invoices to apply payments to when the dues are received in the following year.

L. RECEIVING PAYMENTS ON DUES OR PLEDGES

QBO makes receiving payments on dues easy to record. Go to *+New, Donors, Receive Payment.*

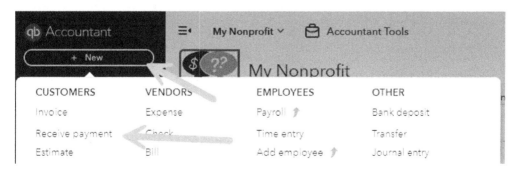

Or got to *Menu, Sales, Invoices, Receive payment* on the appropriate donor's row.

This will then bring up the **Receive Payment** screen. Let's apply a $50 payment from Lisa London from the example above.

If I had gone through the +New menus, I would need to input the donor's name, and all outstanding invoices would appear in the **Outstanding Transactions** list. In most cases, you will apply payments to the oldest invoice first. Just click on the small box to the left of the **Invoice(s)** until the **Amount to Apply** equals the payment amount received.

Fill out the **Payment method** and **Reference number**. **Deposit to** should be Undeposited Funds! If I click on *Receive payment* from the invoice screen, the system will populate the donor name. If a partial payment on the pledge was made, change the amount in the **Amount received box**. For example, if Lisa London only sent in $25, you would change the payment to $25. Next time we pull her outstanding invoices, you will see that this invoice still has a remaining balance of $25.

M. INVOICING AND RECEIPT OF RESTRICTED FUNDS AND GRANTS

If a grant has been awarded or a notice of restricted funds received, you may need to invoice the donor. Do this by going to +*New, Customer, Invoices.*

Select the **Donor** from the drop-down arrow. You will see the list of donors and any related projects or sub-donors they may have. Choose the appropriate project or sub-donor, enter the amount, and choose the **With Donor Restriction** class.

When you receive restricted money that has not been invoiced, go to the **Sales Receipt** or donation screen and enter the receipt with the **Funds with Donor Restriction** class.

Select the sub-donor or project if it is a grant or contract that you will need to report the related expenses. Let's first assume you do not need to report back to the donor. Select **CLASS** to *Funds with Donor Restriction.*

The default descriptions from the items can be changed by typing over them. The more detail entered here, the easier it is to look up information later. You can attach documents detailing the restrictions to the donor's account through the Customer Center.

Next let's go back to the Donor list and learn how to apply a payment received from a grantor set up as a sub-donor. Select *Sales, Donors* from the left menu bar. Type *Best* in the **Search** box. The yearly grants that were created as sub-donors will appear. Select the first *sub-donor.* Pay special attention to which sub-donors there are and which the money received relates to.

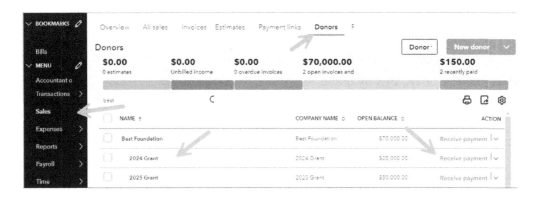

You have arrived at the first year (sub-donor) of the grant. Now select *Receive payment* to enter the check.

The **Received Payment** screen will appear. Enter the amount of the receipt next to the appropriate invoice. Select *Save and close* to return to the transaction list. The Invoices list will show the **Status** as Paid or Partially paid.

If you are using **Projects**, you will receive payments the same way, either through the *Sales, Invoices or Donors* screen or by selecting *+New, Donors, Receive Payment.*

N. MISCELLANEOUS RECEIPTS

Sometimes your organization receives money for miscellaneous receipts like small fundraisers or pamphlet sales that are not related to a particular donor. For these donations, you will set up a generic customer (i.e., Carnival Fundraiser, Pamphlet Sales, or Misc.) and related items (Products/Services). The items link to specific accounts in the chart of accounts in order to record the donations in the correct line on the financial statements.

Miscellaneous receipts can be entered through **Sales Receipt** in the same way as regular donations explained earlier. For the donor name, enter the generic customer and fill out the form the same way you did cash or check receipts above.

Another option is to go to the deposit screen. Go to *+New, Other, Bank Deposit.*

If there are outstanding deposits, they will appear at the top of the deposit screen.

The deposits at the top are the **Sales receipts** and **Invoice payments** we recorded to **Undeposited Funds** earlier.

For this example, there is a deposit of $150 for books sold. Ignore the deposits showing in **Select the payments included in this deposit** area. In the **Add funds to this deposits** section below, you can enter the non-donor related income without setting up customers. Remember to select *Save and close* at the bottom right of the screen when done.

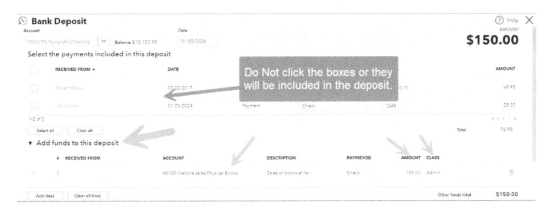

> **DO NOT** *enter donations from specific donors on this screen. Donations must go through invoices or sales receipts, or you will not be able to generate accurate reports by donor name.*

O. PASS-THROUGH COLLECTIONS

Your organization may take up collections for other organizations, like a local food bank or Habitat for Humanity®. A check will be sent to the nonprofit for the amount collected, so you will record them a little differently.

Let's set up a few things first. The organization the donations are to be given to needs to be set up both as a donor and a vendor. Establish a service item for pass-through donations and add to the chart of accounts an **Other Income**-type account for pass-through donations and an **Other Expense** type account for pass-through payments. (As a reminder, you can do this by going to *Gear, Lists, Product & services* or by Adding under the **PRODUCT/SERVICE** column on the Sales Receipt.)

When money is received, choose *Sales Receipt.*

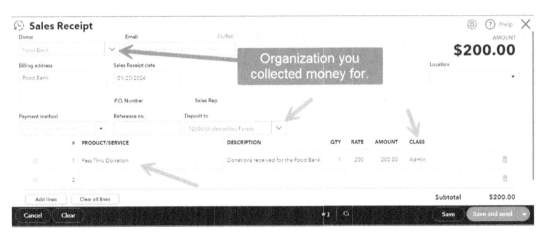

Donor is the organization who should receive the donations. The class is Admin (or Outreach). Select *Pass Thru Donations* as the revenue **Product/Service**. If you have a description in the item, it will appear. You can delete it or add any additional information under the **Description** line. Enter the *Amount* and select *Save & close.*

The above method tracks pass-through donations assuming you usually only have one organization you are collecting for at a time. If you have several organizations you collect money for concurrently, you may wish to set up a separate class called *Pass-Through Donations* and then have sub-classes for each organization.

The total amount due to the other organization must now be set up as a bill to be paid. I'll walk you through that process in the next chapter.

P. UNDEPOSITED FUNDS

I hate to talk like an accountant, but I need to explain what QBO is doing behind the scenes for Undeposited Funds. QBO records the money coming in as revenue based on the account numbers you assigned to the items. In the accounting world, there must be two sides to each entry. Instead of recording the money straight into the **Checking** account, QBO posts the other side of the entry to the **Undeposited Funds** account. The system assumes that after you recorded the money in the accounting system, you've put that day's money in a safe or bank bag along with any other monies yet to be deposited. Think of **Undeposited Funds** as the stack of checks and money you have in that bank bag. Once the deposits are physically made, you tell QBO which checks went into each deposit.

When you are ready to deposit the money, go to +*New, OTHER, Bank deposit.*

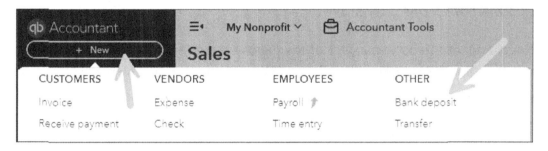

This brings up the **Deposit** screen. At the top, select the **Bank Account** where the deposit was made and the **Date** of the deposit. All sales receipts and payments you had previously entered, but not yet designated as deposited, will appear under **Select Existing Payments**. Choose the items for a particular deposit by clicking the box to the left of the entries included in that deposit. The total of cash and check entries should correspond with the deposits on your bank statement. The top right corner of the screen will show the total of the deposit.

The total of each deposit in the system must equal the total of each deposit submitted to the bank.

If the organization is tracking their checking account with the three subaccounts (unrestricted, temporarily restricted, and permanently restricted), the bookkeeper will need to record the donation as three different deposits—one for each subaccount. The total of all entries should also correspond to the collections totals from the sheet received from the person who collected the funds.

Q. PRINTING A DEPOSIT SLIP

Select *Print* at the bottom center of the deposit screen to print a deposit slip and summary. If you have printable deposit slips, you can print a bank-ready form. The deposit forms are available from Intuit or your bank.

The first time you use a printable deposit slip, select *Setup and alignment* to test the margins and spacing.

Once you are happy with the form setup, select *Print deposit slip and summary.* QBO will automatically save your deposit.

A **Deposit Summary** screen including all of the checks and cash you selected in the deposit screen will appear.

Print the deposit summary and file it with the receipts document received from the financial secretary or treasurer. It will serve as your audit trail.

*Using **Undeposited Funds** makes reconciling your bank account so much easier. It summarizes the receipts deposited together so the total matches the deposit amount on your bank statement. Otherwise, you would have to select individual customer checks on the bank reconciliation screens until they added up to the total deposits.*

R. RECURRING DONATIONS FROM CREDIT CARDS

Organizations are increasingly encouraging donors to use credit cards to pay their pledges. Credit card receipts can be set up for online payments through a third party or through a service within QBO for a fee. You will need to research the fee structure and reports available to determine which makes the most sense for your organization. If you use a third party, you will input the receipt as we discussed above but change the **Payment Method** to the type of credit card. At the end of each month, you would record the credit card charges through a journal entry. I'll explain how to do that in Chapter 11.

If you are using the QBO service, go to the top of the *Menu, Sales, Payment links* and follow the prompts to apply to the service. The system will automatically fill in your company information automatically and ask for additional information.

Here are the rates as of January 2024.

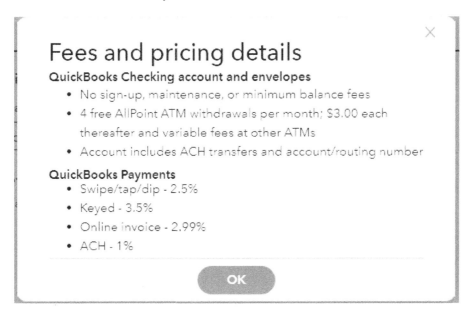

Fees and pricing details

QuickBooks Checking account and envelopes
- No sign-up, maintenance, or minimum balance fees
- 4 free AllPoint ATM withdrawals per month; $3.00 each thereafter and variable fees at other ATMs
- Account includes ACH transfers and account/routing number

QuickBooks Payments
- Swipe/tap/dip - 2.5%
- Keyed - 3.5%
- Online invoice - 2.99%
- ACH - 1%

OK

I recommend comparing them to the rates you are currently paying your credit card processor or PayPal. If they are similar, I recommend switching to QuickBooks Payments as it will save you data entry, processing, and reconciling time. QBO processes the credit card and records the donation and the receipt into your records. Though there are fees, this process makes it much easier to reconcile the money deposited in the bank to the amount recorded in QBO.

If you are using a different payment processor, you will need to pay attention to how the merchant fees are showing in the system. The donations need to be recorded in full and the merchant fees or service charges recorded in an expense account. In Chapter 11, I'll be showing you how the PayPal app feeds into the donations.

Summary

We covered a lot in this chapter, including learning how to:

- Establish basic controls on handling the money coming into the organization
- Enter simple donations
- Handle pledges and invoicing
- Receive payments
- Email acknowledgments
- Save time by setting up recurring invoices
- Determine whether to use projects or sub-donors
- Handle pass-through collections
- Make deposits
- Accept credit card payments

In the next chapter we'll learn how to record the money going out.

9

MONEY OUT—HOW DO I PAY THE BILLS?

A. CASH VS. ACCRUAL METHODS

Now that you know how to record the money coming in, it's time to work on the money going out. Before we get started, I'll need to throw a little accounting terminology at you.

There are two methods to account for expenses and revenues in the accounting world—Cash and Accrual. The cash method is the simplest. The cash is recorded in the financial statements when it is physically received and when the checks are written. The accrual method requires dating the transaction when the income was earned (i.e. when the grant was awarded) or the expense item was purchased, not necessarily when cash changed hands or when a check was written.

For businesses or organizations that pay taxes or are publicly held, the difference is significant. Nonprofit organizations can use either depending on their governing boards and donor or government requirements. Fortunately, QBO allows you to report the information either way.

To illustrate the differences, assume you receive an invoice from a contractor who did repairs to your office on July 31, but you didn't write him a check until August 15. If you enter the invoice with a date of July 31, you can run financial reports for July showing the expense by selecting the accrual method. If you were to run the report using the cash method, the expense would not appear until the August statements.

In case you are wondering why I'm telling you this, I'm going to have you input your bills using the accrual method, so you have both options for reporting.

*The **accrual method** gives you the most accurate financial picture of your nonprofit, showing money you have earned and expenses you have incurred. The **cash basis** gives you a better idea of when the money has come in or gone out. By allowing you to run the reports either way, QBO gives you the best of both worlds.*

B. INTERNAL ACCOUNTING CONTROLS FOR PAYING BILLS

Fraud, theft, and mistakes are as much of a concern with the money going out as they are with the money coming in. Procedures and controls need to be in place to keep phantom employees or fake vendor invoices from being paid. To ensure good stewardship over your organization's money, you will need strong accounting controls as it relates to the money paid out.

Remember the basic rule. If someone has access to the money, he should not have access to the financial records.

The bookkeeper must not be an authorized check signer. I know this sounds nearly impossible for a small organization, but, here again, you may need to utilize the members of the governing board or other volunteers.

Do not enter bills into the system without documentation and approval from someone other than the bookkeeper. This can be the executive director or treasurer. Sometimes the documentation is as simple as a bill from the utility company or a handwritten note asking the volunteer who drove someone to be reimbursed for his gas. If the expense is to be charged to more than one program, the approver should also note this. Most importantly, all bills to be paid must be approved.

The bookkeeper will enter and code the bills into the correct expense categories and programs or grants. He will then print the checks, match them up with the approved documentation, and give them to an authorized check signer. The check signer should assure himself that the payee, address, and amounts agree to the approved documentation and sign the checks. The checks are then mailed, and the documentation filed or scanned.

I recommend you use a voucher-style check. This allows a space for the payee to see what invoice was paid. Your portion of the voucher should be stapled to the approved invoice and filed under the vendor's name. The check signer should never sign a check made out to him. A different signer is required for that.

You will want at least two authorized signers. Besides not allowing a signer to sign his own check, a signer may be unavailable, and the organization will still need to pay their bills. Requiring two signatures over a certain dollar amount is another control, but be aware: with electronic scanning, banks no longer check for two signatures on the checks.

Don't forget about physical controls. Thefts do occur. A member of a cleaning crew once stole some checks from a client of mine and forged them. Keep your checks in a locked drawer or file cabinet, not just a locked office.

C. CONTROLS FOR ELECTRONIC PAYMENTS

Having controls over checks and check writing is good, but now paying bills online and automatic drafts are the norm. No more tracking down envelopes and stamps and running to the post office. However convenient this is, it makes it necessary to implement controls to assure all payments are recorded in the financial statements in a timely manner and no unauthorized payments are made.

You may process payments electronically through QBO. This means one person can set up the vendor, enter the transaction, and send the payment electronically. While this is convenient, it does not separate the person making the entry from the person sending the money. Separate users with limited access will need to be established in the system. I'll explain how to do this in Chapter 15.

Your bank may offer bill payment through their website. If so, you will need to set up separate logins and passwords for the bill payment area and the reporting and downloading area. This is because you want to allow the bookkeeper to see the transactions and download them, while not having access to the money. Additionally, you do not want the person authorizing the payments to be able to manipulate the financial statements. Because each bank or service is different, you will need to work with their professionals to establish your logins and passwords.

If payments can be made directly through a vendor's website, the login and password combination must not be known to the bookkeeper. The bookkeeper will record the payment in QBO, but an authorized check signer should have the login and password combinations. QBO also allows other companies to develop applications that work directly with the system.

D. ENTERING BILLS

It's time to pay some bills. The mail has been opened, the bills approved and coded, and you are now ready to start entering. You will *enter* bills as they come in and *pay* bills when they are due.

As you have noticed in the other areas, there are a couple of ways to access the bills area. One way is to go to *+New, Vendors, Bill.* Clicking *Bill* will take you to a screen to start entering the invoices due.

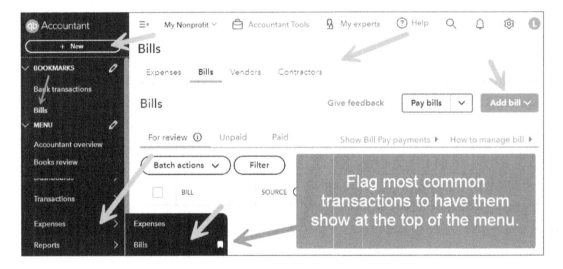

The **Expenses, Bills** tab on the left side menu bar will bring you to the **Bills** entry screen. This screen also allows you to access the screens for Expenses, Vendors, Contractors, and Mileage.

If you are going to pay for something with a check in the future, enter it in the **Bills** screen. If you have already paid for it via credit card or manually wrote the check, enter it as in the **Expense** screen. They are very similar entries; the difference being you can schedule the payment and print checks if you use the **Bills** screen. I'll go through the Expense screen later in the chapter when I explain how to enter credit card charges.

The **Vendors** tab will list all the vendors you have previously entered and any open balances.

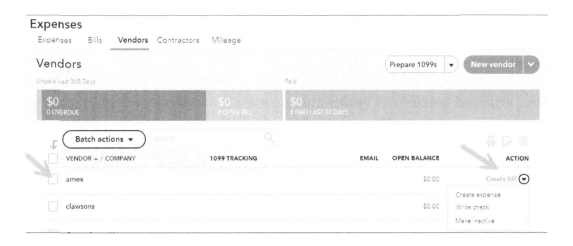

All vendors previously entered are listed. You can also create a **New vendor** using the green button in the upper right corner of the screen. If there are no open invoices for a particular vendor, you will see a **Create bill** link. If there are open invoices, the link will say **Make payment.**

Select the down arrow next to **Create bill** or **Make payment** for additional actions. I go over the **Create expense** and **Write check** options when we talk about paying bills later in the chapter. For now, let's focus on entering bills.

There are also **Batch actions** on the left that allow you to make the vendor inactive or email them.

Whether you go through the *+New* menu on the home page or click *Create bill* for a specific vendor in the **Vendor Center**, an entry screen for **Bill** will appear. It has a very similar layout to the Invoice/Pledge screen.

If you had selected *Create bill* from the Vendor Center, that name will appear on the entry screen. Otherwise, you can start typing a vendor name and select from the drop-down menu.

Once you have selected the **Vendor**, the address is automatically entered. Input the date of the invoice in the **Bill date** box. This is important in order to run reports on an accrual basis. The **Bill no.** should be the invoice number on the bill. If there is no invoice number, I like to use the date. At the top right, **BALANCE DUE** will update as you enter the details of the invoice. If you designated vendor-specific terms during setup, QBO will calculate the **Due date** automatically. If you didn't, you can use the drop-down arrow in the **Terms** field and select the appropriate date or leave it blank. Having an accurate due date helps the management of the cash flow. You have the option to add **Tags** to the bill.

The bottom half of the screen is where you will enter the individual line items of the invoice. There are two sections: **Category details** and **Item details**. The **Category details** section has you charge the expense directly to an account in your chart of accounts. As I explained in Chapter 7, **Items (Products/Services)** are useful to track the details you don't necessarily need on the financial statements. If you choose an Item, the account that was linked to the item will be charged in your financial statements.

Under **Category details**, you will enter separate lines for charges to accounts and their related classes. For example, the telephone bill could be charged to two different programs. In the first line under **CATEGORY,** select an account for the first item on the invoice. Start to type in the word or account number, and the drop-down menu will give you options. Next, in the **DESCRIPTION** area, explain why the money was spent. Input the dollar amount charged to the first program under **AMOUNT**.

The **BILLABLE** option is only needed if there are reimbursable expenses that can be billed back to a donor. Use this only if you invoice donors for specific purchases. If the item was purchased for a grant or contract that needs to be tracked, select the *Sub-donor or Project* from the **DONOR** drop-down menu. The last column is the **CLASS**. There should be a class (think program) designated for every expense item. If it is related to a grant or other restriction, use the With Donor Restriction class.

There is also a place to add a **Memo** and to upload a scan of the bill in **Attachments**. Finally, you can *Save and new, Save and close, or Save and schedule payment*. If you choose to schedule the payment, a screen will appear asking you to sign up for QuickBooks bill pay. It allows you to ACH payments to vendors instead of having to print checks and the system automatically matches the payment to the bill. If you have five or less payments a month, the service is free. For up to 40 payments, the current cost is $15 per month.

E. BEGINNING ACCOUNTS PAYABLE BALANCE

If your organization has used the accrual method of accounting, you may have a balance in your accounts payable as of your start date. If so, each of the vendor invoices needs to be entered into the system with an invoice date of the prior year. For example, if your beginning balance includes a $200 bill from a printing company from December of the prior year, enter it as a bill with a December invoice date. This will allow your beginning balance to reflect the correct amount in accounts payable.

F. UPLOADING BILLS

A very handy feature of QBO is the ability to upload a bill from a pdf file. For example, if you receive email versions of any of your bills, you can upload it into QBO, and the system will scan it and upload it for you to review before posting.

To do this go to *Menu, Expenses, Bills, Add bill, Upload from computer.*

The system will take a couple of minutes to import the bill. Once the file is uploaded, click on the *For Review* tab to see all scanned bills. Hit *Review* to open, adjust, and post. The system will show the bill next to the line items so you can easily check each box. **Don't forget to check the CLASS!**

If it recognizes the vendor, it will code it to the account in the vendor record. If it doesn't recognize the vendor, it will ask you to designate which vendor or to set up a new one. Double check that the amount and account is correct and *Save*.

The uploaded scan will be attached, and the bill automatically be moved to the **Unpaid** tab. If the bill is set up on auto-pay and you are using bank feeds (Chapter 11), you will be able to match the Unpaid bill to the payment when it is downloaded from the bank. The bill will then move to the **Paid** tab.

 You can drag multiple bills over at the same time for the system to process. Then check the For Review tab to review.

Don't worry if you accidentally upload the same invoice twice; the system will highlight it and make it easy to delete.

In Chapter 15, I'll be explaining how to use the mobile app. It has a **Snap Receipt** option that easily uploads bills and expenses for you to review and record.

G. EDITING AND DELETING BILLS

Whether it is a bill you entered or one that was uploaded, you may need to make some changes. As I looked at the bills under the **Unpaid** tab, I noticed in the bill that was uploaded above, the system read Tax on the bill and assumed Sales Tax Payable. This should be a property tax bill, so let's change it.

To remedy this situation, I need to click anywhere on the line of the highlighted bill with the error. This will bring up the bill as it was entered.

You can now edit the amounts, expense accounts, or classes. In this case, I need to change the **Category** in line one from Sales Tax Payable to Property Taxes. Then select *Save and close* or *Save and schedule payment.*

If this bill was a duplicate, you would need to delete it. At the bottom of the bill screen, select *More* and then *Delete*. A warning box will appear asking if you are sure. If you are, select *Yes*, and you will go back to the list of transactions for that vendor.

You can also access recent bills by pulling up the **Bill** screen (*+New, VENDORS, Bill*) and clicking on the clock icon in the upper left corner.

A list of the most recently entered and edited bills will appear. Click on any of them to edit or review.

H. RECURRING BILLS

Your organization probably has some bills that need to be paid each month, like rent, utilities, etc. QBO allows you to set up recurring bills and then reminds you to pay them. The process is similar to setting up recurring membership dues. Got to *+New, Vendors, Bill* to bring up the **Bill** screen. Select *Make recurring* in the bottom center or go to *Menu, Expenses, Bills, Add Bill, Create recurring bill.*

Either way will take you to the **Recurring Bill** template. If you have just entered a bill for a vendor, the system will default to the last information entered for that vendor. You can make changes to any field before saving this template.

There are three template types relating to reminders, and they are found in the **Type** drop-down menu next to the vendor name. The first option, **Scheduled**, is the handiest if the amount stays the same each month (like rent). It will automatically enter the bill into your accounts to be paid. The second, **Reminder**, will add it to a reminders list that will pop up when you sign into QBO. The third option, **Unscheduled**, allows you to set up the memorized transaction but not remind you. This is used for items without a set schedule.

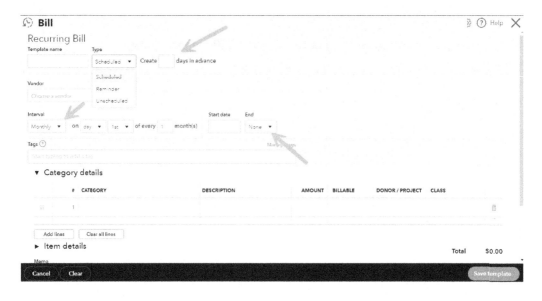

Next, the **Create X days in advance** tells QBO when to put it in the Accounts Payable list. This should be determined by how often you pay bills. If your organization pays weekly, seven days should be sufficient.

You need to determine how often you want the bill to be added. If you were entering a utility bill, select *Monthly* in the **Interval** section. Next you need to let the system know the **Start date**, i.e. the date of the next invoice, and when it should **End**. The **End** menu gives three options: **None, By**, and **After**. The **By** option allows you to enter an end date; the **After** option goes by number of occurrences. By selecting *After* with *12 occurrences*, the system will keep generating these bills monthly for the next 12 consecutive months.

If you pay the same amount for the bill each month, like rent, then go ahead and input the amount of rent. But for bills that vary (water or electricity, for example), leave the amount blank. Select *Save template* when you are done.

You can always find all **Recurring Transactions** from the **Gear Icon** under **Lists**. From here, you can edit or delete any transaction template.

Before you add too many recurring bills, read through **Chapter 11 Bank Transactions**. If you have bills on automatic drafts, you can save lots of time using the Rules through Bank Feeds instead of setting up recurring bills.

I.   ENTER CREDIT CARD CHARGES

Some of the organization's employees may have a credit card in the organization's name. The charges need to be supported by receipts, entered into the system, and the bill paid. There are a few basic approaches. The first option is to hand the employee a copy of the bill when it arrives and require them to fill out an expense report detailing what each expense was for. The receipts are then attached to the expense report and submitted to a supervisor for approval. The approved expense report is given to the bookkeeper to enter as a bill or match to the **Bank Transaction (**Chapter 11).

The second choice is to have the employee hand in receipts for approval as they use the credit card. The treasurer then knows how much cash will be needed to pay the bill when it arrives.

The third option is to have the employee save scanned receipts in a Google drive or email a picture or scan of the receipt to the bookkeeper to send to QBO via a dedicated email. I'll go through those steps in the next section.

To enter them manually, go to *Menu, Expenses, Expenses.*

Choose the **Payee.** Set the **Payment account** to the credit card. Enter the expense and be sure to use a Class. Attach a scan of the receipt if possible. If you are billed each month to the card, choose **Make recurring.** *Save* when finished.

Handling Receipts for Expenses

QBO allows you to set up a dedicated email account to use for importing receipts into the system. Go to *Menu, Transactions, Receipts.*

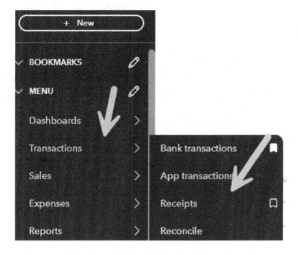

A screen will appear giving you three options to upload the receipts.

You have already seen how to upload them to the computer via the **drag and drop**. If you click on the **Google Drive,** the system will step you through tying your google drive account to QBO. Any receipts saved to that folder in the drive will be uploaded for review. The third possibility is to have a dedicated email address. **Please note:** any bills you send to this special email must come from the email address you signed into QBO with.

Set up receipt forwarding

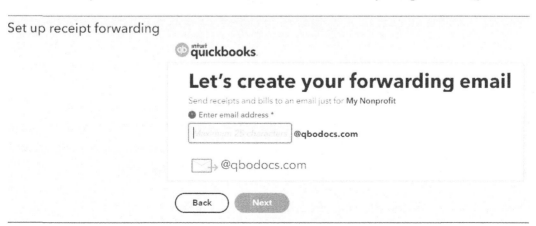

J. PAYING BILLS

You have entered all the bills and are now ready to cut the checks, but bills are not necessarily due at the same time. I'll show you how to select which bills you want to pay. Go to the *+New, Expenses, Bills, Pay Bills*. The **Pay Bills** screen will list all bills due by a certain date or, if you prefer, all bills.

Check the **Payment account** to ascertain that the correct checking account is being charged. The default bank account is the last account used when paying bills. This can be overridden using the drop-down arrow. It will display the current system account balance (not the bank balance). **Payment date** is the date you want printed on the checks. The **Starting check no.** will default to the next check in the series from any earlier printings but can be overridden. The system will tell you how much money will be needed in the top right corner.

The **Filter** option allows you to display invoices by a range of due dates and/or by vendors. If a large number of bills appears on the screen, you may want to sort them. Do this by double-clicking on the title of the column you want sorted, i.e. sort alphabetically by vender by clicking on the **Payee** title or sort by largest to smallest amounts by choosing the **Open Balance** column.

Choose the bills to be paid by selecting the small box to the left of the bill. You can choose all or some of the bills to pay. At the bottom of the screen, the system shows you the current cash balance and the impact of all the bills selected.

Once you have selected the bills you would like to pay, *Save and print.*

At the bottom of is the **Print setup** to assure the check prints properly. If you select it, QBO will prompt you to do some test prints on a blank sheet of paper. Hold the sample up to the light over a check to see if everything is lined up before you start to print. This is also a good time to test whether you need to place checks face up or face down in your printer. I do this by placing an **X** on the blank sheet and see what side it prints on.

If the lines do not align properly, choose *No, continue setup.* A screen will appear allowing you to change margins. Run another test page, and when you are happy with the test check, select *Yes, I'm finished with the setup.* The good news is you only need to test your setup the first time you print checks. When you receive a new box of checks, I recommend doing this again, just to play it safe.

This takes you back to the **Print Checks** screen. Think of this as a holding place for checks ready to be printed. Enter the **Starting check no.** To print the checks for the two bills we selected above, choose *Preview and print.*

The **Print preview** screen will appear.

If the blank checks are ready in the printer, select *Print.* The system will bring up a dialog box asking to verify that the checks printed correctly.

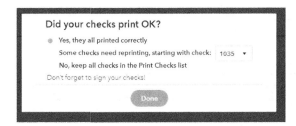

The system will default to **YES**. If the checks printed correctly, choose *Done*. If the printer jammed and the last check is unreadable, QBO makes it easy to reprint the check. Simply select *Some checks need reprinting* and choose the check number. Place new checks in the printer and click *Done* to reprint the checks.

K. WRITE CHECKS

I'm sure you have been in the situation that all of your checks have been printed, but a worker steps in and wants his check today. Rather than enter this as a bill that needs to be paid in the future, you can write (enter) a check directly from the **Check** screen.

Go to *+New, Vendors, Check*. The **Check** screen will appear.

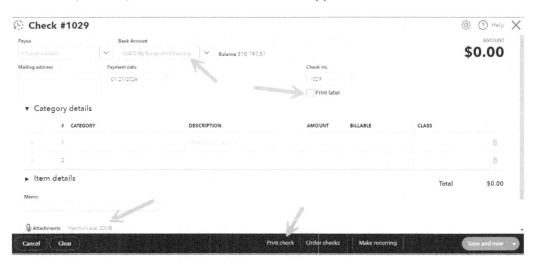

Notice this screen has similar fields to the **Bill** screen, including **Category details** and **Item details**. The check entry screen will say **Check no.** at the top followed by the defaulted next available check number. Don't worry if that isn't the check number you will be using. If you click **Print later**, you can assign a different number when you print the check.

 QBO screens can look very similar. Always check the screen title at the top left to be sure you are in the correct screen.

Payment date will default to today's date. Make sure the correct checking account is showing. The account **Balance** will show the amount QBO has recorded in the bank before you write the check.

Key in the vendor's name in the **Choose a payee** area. The options under this drop-down include all vendors, customers, and employees who have been set up previously. This will be a longer list than you saw under **Bills**, where only the vendors are listed. If the payee has been input before, scroll down until you find her name listed as a vendor.

*If this vendor is new and may need a 1099, be sure to click the **Track payments for 1099** under **Additional info** in the New Vendor screen.*

If the vendor is an independent contractor, you will need his Federal Identification Number or Social Security Number. I explain the difference between employees and independent contractors in detail in my books, Church Accounting—The How-To Guide for Small & Growing Churches and Nonprofit Accounting for Treasurers, Volunteers, and Bookkeepers.

To print the check immediately, make certain the **Print later** is NOT selected. Select *Print check* at the bottom of the screen. The **Print Checks** screen will appear. The check you are printing should be the only one selected. Put the check in the printer, type in the check number, and select *Preview and print*.

*Employee and donor reimbursements can be paid through the **Check** screen. If you use the **Bill** screen to input their invoices, you will need to set up vendor accounts with a different name than their donor or employee name. One option is to put a small "v" after the name to differentiate (i.e. **Smith, J** is the donor and **Smith, J v** is the vendor account).*

L. HANDWRITTEN CHECKS

Sometimes you may need to write a check by hand and enter it into the system later. You will do this through the **Check** option. The same fields are required for entry. The only difference is to enter a check number manually.

Deselect the **Print later** box and input the check number from the handwritten check. The rest of the information is entered as before. Then *Save and close*, and the check is recorded.

Any account set up with a credit card account type will be available from the drop-down arrow. Choose the credit card you are working with. **Payment date** will default to today and can be changed to the date on the receipt if desired. Select the type of credit card you are using from the drop-down menu of the **Payment method** box.

Next, break down the expenditure by expense account under the **Category details** section. Type in any description that may be useful. Enter the **Amount** and **Class** for each charge. A very handy feature is the ability to scan the receipt and attach it to the entry (Great way to find the support during audit season!). Scroll to the bottom to see the paperclip icon. Clicking the box will bring up a menu box to select the scanned receipts you wish to attach. When you are finished, select *Save and new* to enter the next receipt or *Save and close* to finish.

M. PAYING THE CREDIT CARD BILL

When it is time to pay the credit card bill, you will use the **Check** screen. Go to *+New, Vendors, Check*.

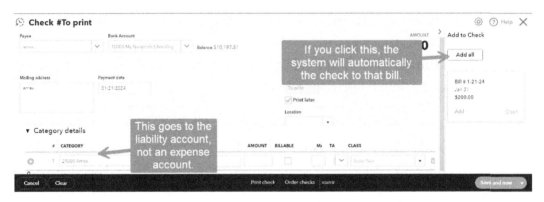

Enter the credit card vendor and select the checking account that the check or draft will come from. The **CATEGORY** is not an expense, but the credit card account in the general ledger, usually a 2xxx series number.

Alternatively, you could select the previously added individual bills or the **Add all** on the right side bar. This will move them to the Check Categories. Make sure the total agrees to the credit card statement and click *Save and close*.

N. CREDITS RECEIVED FROM VENDORS OR ON CREDIT CARD

Credits are often received from vendors or your credit card. These most often occur when you return an item. The vendor issues a credit to the account, lowering the amount due. You will need to enter this credit before you pay the vendor.

Go to *+New, Vendors, Vendor Credit*.

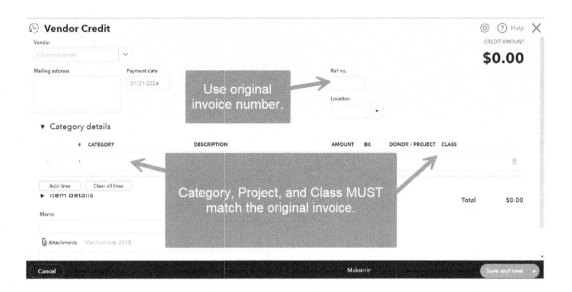

Enter the vendor's name, the credit number or the invoice number it is to be applied against, and the amount. Then enter the same expense account and class of original invoice. Select *Save and new* or *Save and close*.

If you have an open balance with this vendor, when you click inside the **CREDIT APPLIED** box on the **Pay Bills** screen, you will see the credit listed below the blank box.

Simply type in the amount of the credit you wish to apply; the system will adjust the amount due and then write the checks.

To issue a credit for a credit card, go to *+New, Vendors, Credit Card Credit* and follow the same procedures.

Summary

This chapter covered handling the outflow of money. You learned how to:

- Understand the cash vs. accrual methods of accounting for bills
- Set up internal accounting controls for paying bills
- Enter, edit, and delete bills
- Upload bill scans
- Enter the beginning accounts payable balance
- Set up recurring bills
- Pay bills via online payments, and checks
- To enter expenses paid by credit card manually
- Pay the credit card bill
- Record credits received from vendors

This has been a long, detailed chapter. Take a break and I'll explain the payroll options in QBO and how to enter them in the next chapter.

10

PAYROLL

There are numerous ways nonprofits prepare payroll. Most use an outside service that takes care of all the tax and reporting requirements and allows for direct deposits. Others use an accountant to handle it for them. Some prepare their payroll themselves.

QuickBooks offers payroll services that will link directly into your company file. This will save some data entry time, so when you are evaluating prices and services of QuickBooks Payroll and other outside services, please keep this in mind. Here is a chart showing QuickBooks Payroll options.

Please note, I am not associated with QuickBooks, nor do I express an opinion on which payroll service is best suited for your organization. Similar options are available from other payroll services, and many have apps that will interface with QBO.

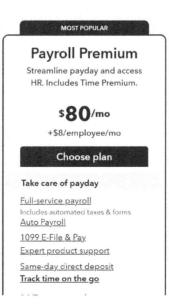

Payroll Core	MOST POPULAR	**Payroll Elite**
Pay your team and get payroll taxes done for you. Time not included.	**Payroll Premium** Streamline payday and access HR. Includes Time Premium.	Access on-demand experts and tax protection. Includes Time Elite.
$**45**/mo	$**80**/mo	$**125**/mo
+$6/employee/mo	+$8/employee/mo	+$10/employee/mo
Choose plan	Choose plan	Choose plan
Take care of payday	**Take care of payday**	**Take care of payday**
Full-service payroll Includes automated taxes & forms	Full-service payroll Includes automated taxes & forms	Full-service payroll Includes automated taxes & forms
Auto Payroll	Auto Payroll	Auto Payroll
1099 E-File & Pay	1099 E-File & Pay	1099 E-File & Pay
Expert product support	Expert product support	Expert product support
Next-day direct deposit	Same-day direct deposit	Same-day direct deposit
	Track time on the go	**Expert setup**

*For additional information about the details surrounding church payroll issues, please consider my book, **Church Accounting: The How-To Guide for Small & Growing Churches**. There are three chapters covering payroll, including the intricacies of minister's payroll, how to calculate payroll, and how to file the reports.*

O. ENTERING EMPLOYEES AND CONTRACTORS

QuickBooks groups **Employees** and **Independent Contractors** under the **Payroll** side menu. If a worker may be considered an independent contractor (see my blog post at https://accountantbesideyou.com/blogs/quicktips/who-is-an-independent-contractor-for-a-nonprofit-or-church for more details), select *Menu, Payroll,* and *Add an employee.*

If you haven't signed up for QuickBooks Payroll, there will be a pop-up box warning you to wait to add the employees after signing up. If you aren't signing up for their services, select *Not right now* to continue.

The top of the form looks remarkably similar to the Donor and Vendor forms with spaces for names, addresses, preferred name for checks, etc. Additionally, the Employee form will have an area for their social security number (SSN), employee number, hire date, and cost and billable rates. You may wish to use these for grant tracking and reporting purposes.

If you are using QuickBooks Payroll service, they will email the employee and have them enter their personal information. If you are not using the service, you will need to enter it yourself.

You may also add any independent contractors here.

Select *Add a contractor* and a screen requesting the contractor's email will appear.

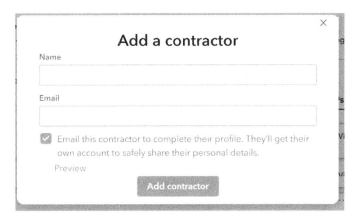

QuickBooks will send them an email that allows the contractor to set up an account with QuickBooks (that can also be used for their other clients) and to enter their personal data. This allows you not to have to hold theirW-9 with the SSN or EIN in your paper files and lessens the likelihood of data entry errors. After they fill in their data, it will populate on the Contractors screen and allow you to pay them directly from there.

The **Contractor** screen also lets you see the last payment, so you can check the date and amount before paying the current bill. The system will also prepare the 1099s at year end, which is a great time saver.

Without the payroll service, once the employee or contractor is added, you can pay them via **Checks** (but the system will not calculate the taxes for you), track their time via apps, and bill them to grants, if appropriate

P. USING JOURNAL ENTRIES TO RECORD PAYROLL

I will walk you through the most common approach to payroll: how to record the payroll from an outside service. Recording payroll can be done via a journal entry or through the **Check** screen. First, I'll explain the journal entry option. If you will recall, you used the journal entry approach to record your beginning balances. You will now use it to record each period's payroll.

The first thing I like to do is design a spreadsheet for the journal entry. This is an extra step, but it assures that once I have all of the allocations completed, the entry will balance.

	A	B	C	D	E
4					
5	Description	Account	Class	Debit	Credit
6	Total Gross Pay	Salaries	Research	5,000.00	
7	Total Gross Pay	Salaries	Education	3,000.00	
8	Total Gross Pay	Salaries	Mangement	4,000.00	
9	Employer Liabilities	Payroll Tax Expense	Research	2,000.00	
10	Employer Liabilities	Payroll Tax Expense	Education	400.00	
11	Employer Liabilities	Payroll Tax Expense	Mangement	752.00	
12	Benefit Contributions Withheld	Other Withholding Liability	Unrestricted		500.00
13	Non-Direct Deposit Check	Cash	Unrestricted		1,680.00
14	Net Pay Allocations	Cash	Unrestricted		10,248.00
15	Employee Tax Withholding	Cash	Unrestricted		1,572.00
16	Employer Liabilities	Cash	Unrestricted		1,152.00
17	Totals			$ 15,152.00	$ 15,152.00
18					

Starting from the bottom, this entry assumes the payroll service has electronically pulled the net pay ($10,248), the employee tax withholdings ($1,572), and the employer liabilities ($1,152) out of the cash account in separate amounts. It also reflects a check written to an employee that did not use direct deposit ($1,680). This is important to list separately as it will clear the bank as a check.

The Benefit Contributions Withheld ($500) went into a liability account as the organization will need to write a check to the benefit company for that withholding. The tax expenses did not have to go to a liability account because the payroll service has already withdrawn the money. If your payroll service does not pay the taxes on your behalf, you would need to record those into liability accounts and then write the appropriate checks.

 Look at your bank statement to see how the payroll service pulls the money out of your cash account. Then design your journal entry to match, which will make reconciling the bank account easier.

For example, if the payroll service charges your checking account with three amounts each month—net pay, employee withholding, and payroll taxes—you will want to assure that your journal entry credits (reduces) the bank account with those three numbers separately, not one complete payroll number.

To enter the payroll entry, go to +*New, Other, Journal Entry*.

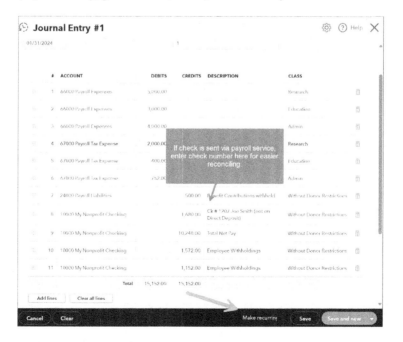

As you key in the account numbers and amounts, please note the system does not require you to use the lowest sub-account on this screen. You will need to be extra careful that you are using the correct account, especially if you are using sub-accounts to track restricted cash.

The gross pay needs to be allocated to the correct accounts and classes. If some of the payroll time should be charged to a grant or contract, select the correct **Sub-donor (grantee)** in the **Name** column for that amount. If the reports from your payroll service do not group the employees by program, ask your payroll representative if that can be arranged. Having their reports already total the dollars by program makes entering the journal entry much easier.

 All expense items, including payroll, must have a designated class. This is how the expenses are allocated to programs.

For any payroll that will not be direct deposited, record the check number in the **DESCRIPTION** to make reconciling the bank account easier. If your payroll is consistent, consider **Make recurring** to have the system record it automatically each month. You will need to edit the entry for the actual data, but it will save data entry time.

Q. ENTERING PAYROLL THROUGH THE CHECK ENTRY SCREEN

The other way to enter payroll from the outside service is through the **Check** screen. This is in lieu of the journal entry. You must be very careful that each bank draft item is treated as a separate check. Set up a vendor called **Payroll** and record the first check for the net pay.

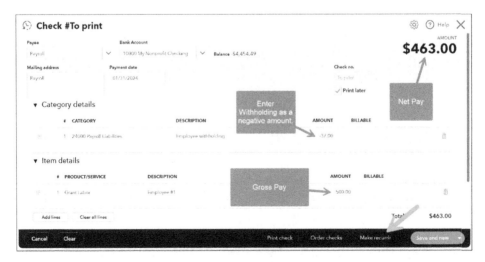

Enter the employee gross pay under either **Category details** in the payroll account or under the **Item details** section if you have a service set up for a grant. Either way, be sure the **Class** is correct and code to a **Donor/Project** if allocated to a grant. Employee withholdings are coded to the Payroll Withholdings account with a **negative** sign in front of the amount. This is to make the check equal the net pay the employees actually received.

You would then write checks for any drafts and for the non-direct deposit amount. If your payroll stays fairly consistent, use **Make recurring** and edit the checks for the following pay periods.

R. PAYING THE BENEFIT CONTRIBUTION

There is one more thing to do before we finish up the payroll. We need to pay any benefit contribution that was withheld. You will do this through the **Check** screen.

Enter the name of the benefit provider, but under **Category details**, select the liability account charged in the payroll entry. When finished, *Save and close*. This should now zero out the liability account.

S. TRACKING TIME FOR PROJECTS

Projects and grants may have different requirements for tracking employee's time. If you only need the total dollars and not number of hours worked, using the methods shown earlier in this chapter are sufficient. If, however, you need to track actual hours worked, you can use the **Time** option on the **Menu,** but realize it will cost another $20 per month. There are other apps to integrate with QBO or you can enter the hours manually.

To enter them manually, go to the left menu and click on *Projects*. Select the grant you need to add hours to and a screen with a snapshot of income and expenses for that project appears. There are also tabs for **Transactions, Time Activity Reports,** and **Attachments**. In the upper right corner, select the *Add to project* (green button), *Time*.

A list of employees and contractors will appear. Choose the one whose time you are recording. The next screen will have a place to enter the total time spent by day or you can specify the start and end times.

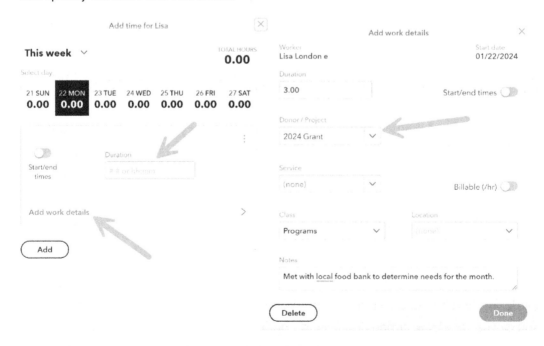

For each time entry, you may select **Add work details**. A new screen will appear where you can enter the **Project, Service, Class,** and **Location** (if used). This is also the place you can notate the purpose of the time spent. Select Billable if required.

Hit **Done** to continue to enter more time. Now when I go back to the Project screen, I can see the hours by employee charged to this project and the related costs.

Summary

In this chapter you learned the basics of the **Employees** options including how to:

- Invite contractors and employees to enter their personal data
- Use journal entries to record payroll
- Enter payroll through the check entry screen
- Paying the benefit contribution
- How to track time for projects

In the next chapter, I'll show you how to reconcile your bank and credit card accounts.

11

BANK TRANSACTIONS & RECONCILIATIONS

n the last few chapters, you have learned how to manually receive donations and pay bills in QBO. Next, I will show you how to utilize QBO's **Bank Transactions** function to save time in data entry and reconciliations. (This was called **Bank Feeds** in the desktop and earlier QBO versions.) I highly recommend connecting every bank, investment, and credit card account you have. You can even connect your PayPal account to automatically download entries.

A. BANKING

The bank transactions and bank rules features in QBO allow you to connect your bank, credit card, and payment processing accounts to QBO. You can take a look at the **Banking** screen in the TestDrive sample company to see what this looks like at https://qbo.intuit. com/redir/testdrive. If you are already logged into your QBO account, you may need to open an InPrivate or Incognito window or go to a different browser. Go to the left side menu and select *Banking*.

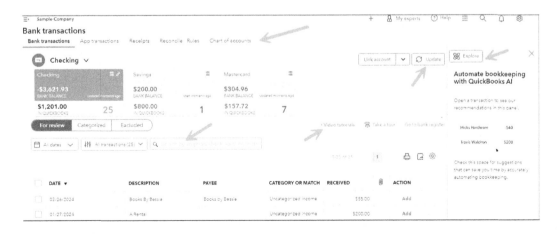

Along the top you will see several tabs, **Bank transactions, App transactions, Receipts, Reconcile, Rules,** and **Chart of accounts**.

The **Bank transaction** tab displays your connected accounts and allows you to automate the assignment of account numbers to each transaction by using predefined assumptions and rules. For example, you may have your electrical bill automatically debited from your bank account. When QBO sees a transaction with electricity or power in the description, it will suggest that this transaction belongs to utilities.

The **App Transactions** tab will show transactions from various apps you can connect to your Quickbooks account. This is primarily used for sales channels. I explained the **Receipts** tab in Chapter 9 on bills. The **Reconcile** tab will be used at month-end to reconcile your bank and credit card accounts. **Rules** are designed to save data entry when auto payments are downloaded, so you can bill them to the correct programs and accounts. The **Chart of accounts** is the listed on the final tab. There you can **View register** to see individual transactions in each account.

Let's go over the **Banking Transactions** screen. At the top right are three buttons, **Link account**, **Update**, and **Explore**. Press *Link Account* to go to a **Connect an account** screen. This will link each of your accounts to their financial institutions and show the transactions. The drop-down arrow beside it will allow you to do **Upload from file, Manage connections, or Order checks**.

Update will have the system pull new transactions from your linked accounts. If it sees a transaction has already been downloaded, it will not duplicate it. **Explore** is a new feature that uses AI to give recommendations on how to code transactions. Play around with this as you are working with transactions and see if it will help you.

Along the main area you will see blocks set up for each of the accounts you have linked.

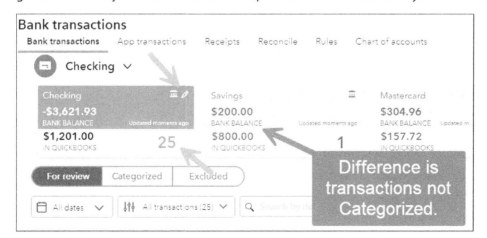

If you click on the small pencil icon, you can edit the sign in info and account info for your online banking account. This needs to be done if you have changed the passwords or the bank has updated their system.

The blocks show two balances, **BANK BALANCE** and **IN QUICKBOOKS.** The account currently selected is blue, and only the transactions in that account are displayed. The number in the right corner of the book shows the number of transactions that need reviewed.

The dark line below indicates the **For Review** tab is selected. These transactions are NOT in QBO yet. The next tab is **Categorized**. These are recent items that have already been accepted and posted into your financial records. The **Excluded** tab list transactions that were not approved to be included in your records. You can also access the check register for that account using **Go to bank register** on the upper right corner.

Below those tabs are boxes that allow you to sort the transactions. **All transactions (#)** lists all of the transactions downloaded and tells you how many there are available for review or have been categorized or excluded (depending on which screen you are on). The drop-down arrow lets you sort in more detail, including which transactions have been **Recognized (#)**. Clicking on it will only show the transactions that you have set up rules for or QuickBooks recognizes from earlier entries. I recommend going to the Recognized area first as you can usually approve these quickly and leave the unmatched items listed for any necessary research.

You'll see the **Date, Description** (usually from the bank), **Payee** (if you've set up a rule) **Category** (chart of account number), and amount **Spent** or **Received**. In the right column is the **Action** area. The actions will be either **Match, Add, or View.**

Match indicates QBO has identified what it believes is a matching payment for an existing open invoice. Click *Match* if you agree that this transaction is related to a previously entered invoice and it should be added to QBO. This will apply the payment to the invoice (or the receipt to a donor invoice).

If you have previously told QBO how to code a particular transaction, the system will "guess" that account number and give you the Add option. For any payments QBO does not recognize how to match, the system will label as an Uncategorized Expense. By clicking on the line, you can view the downloaded details and the related options. Select the correct account from the chart of accounts. If the amount should be split between accounts, The Split button will allow you to charge the expense to more than one account. Always be sure to add the Class!

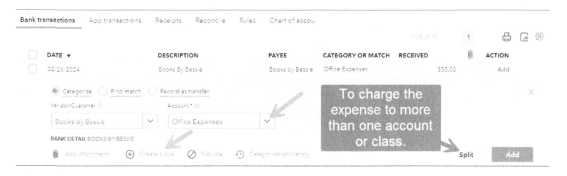

Along the bottom of the screen, you may Add attachment, Create a rule, Exclude, and see the Categorization history. Add will record the entry after you have selected the correct category or categories for it.

Occasionally you will see View as an option. This means the system has found two possible transactions the download could be matching. Click on view and select the correct one or edit as appropriate.

B. CONNECTING YOUR ACCOUNTS

Let's go back to the Bank screen in your QBO account. Select *Transactions, Banking*. If there are already accounts connected, you will see the Bank screen similar to the one we worked with in the previous section. Select *Add account*. If there are no accounts already set up, you will see a screen similar to the one below.

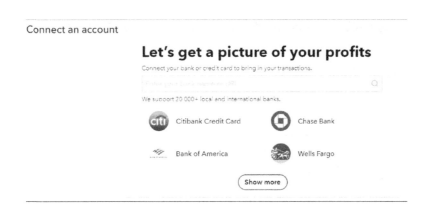

QBO has a relationship with most major banks in the US. Select the logo of your bank, if it is listed. If not, start typing in the bank name. The system will give you a drop-down list of options. If your bank is not listed, they may not have an agreement with QBO to connect your account, but I would call the bank just to make sure.

After selecting your bank, log in using your same username and password you use to access your account online on the bank's website.

This allows QBO to retrieve your account information from online banking. Every account you have at this bank will appear in the list; select any accounts used by your organization, clicking the box to the left of it.

Next, choose the corresponding **QuickBooks Account** (think chart of accounts) for each account. The account may already be in your chart of accounts, or if it is new, you can create it by selecting *Add new* from the drop-down menu.

You can download up to 0, 7, 30, or 90 days of checks, deposits, and other transactions. When you are done, click *Connect* to go back to the **Bank** screen.

1. Understanding Bank transactions

After an account is connected to your QBO Company, income and expense transactions will automatically be imported into the Bank area for review. They will not be entered into QBO until you match them to open invoices or chart of account numbers and accept them.

You will still create invoices (Chapter 8) for dues and pledges and enter bills and write checks (Chapter 9). We learned in Chapters 8 and 9 how to enter these transactions manually and by recurring transactions. For example, you entered the phone bill and paid it by check. When the check clears the bank, it will download with your bank feed, and QBO will **Match** it with the check in the system.

Deposits will be downloaded as lump sums from the bank. If you have used the Undeposited Funds option and grouped your individual donations into deposits, the system should match them automatically.

If you have automatic drafts for normal recurring expenses, the system will try to "guess" the account if there isn't an invoice already set up. To take the guessing out, you can set up **Rules**.

2. Understanding Rules

Bank rules are predefined conditions that tell QBO how to categorize transactions. Rules scan bank items for particular details and then assign specific payees and categories to them, saving you time matching the bank information to your accounts.

You can add and edit rules by going to the *Rules* tab on the **Bank Transactions** screen. In the upper right-hand corner, you will find a box labeled **New rule**. Click on the down arrow to see **Export rules** and **Import rules**.

The rules are based on the text downloaded from the bank, the description, and/or the amount. Start by selecting *New rule* to see a screen similar to this one.

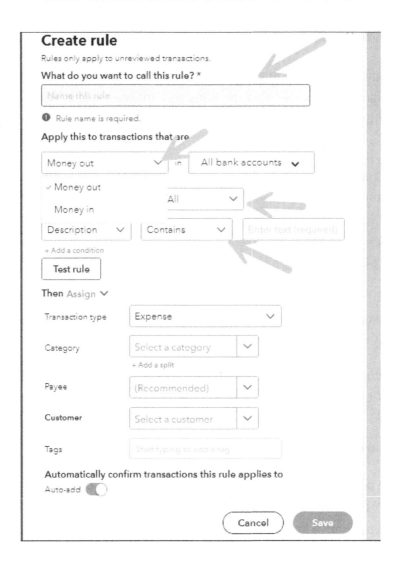

Assign a **Rule name**. Keep it simple enough to remind you what the rule does. The **For** option is **Money in** or **Money out**. If the rule is for a deposit, use Money in; if for a vendor, use Money out. The **All bank accounts** box has a drop-down menu allowing you to select which account this rule should apply to. For example, if all checks are paid from a general operating checking account, that is the only one that should be selected for any vendor rules. If it is a rule related to credit card charges, you may want to select only the MasterCard option.

The next line defines whether the rule will be run when **all** or **any** of the conditions are met. You are allowed up to five conditions per rule. The next three boxes set the conditions. First select whether the system should look for the **Bank text, Description**, or the **Amount** from the downloaded data. Then choose whether it **Contains,** reflects

Exactly, or **Doesn't contain** the information you key into the third box.

The **Transaction type** will tell the system whether to record it as an expense, check, transfer, or deposit. Select the **Payee** from the drop-down list and the **Category** from your chart of accounts. Be sure to include the **Class** on every rule. The **Split** button allows you to allocate the expense to more than one account.

Click *Save* when done, and the new rule will be added to your list of rules. Though the set up takes a bit of effort, it is rather easy and saves you time recording future entries

Posting Feed Transactions

Transactions imported from your bank account are **not** automatically posted to QBO. You must review and accept each transaction to post it.

A recognized transaction will have a match—a rule has been applied, or QBO uses categories from related transactions. But the system doesn't record the match. You still must say it is okay to post either individually or click the top box to the left of DATE to select all of the transactions listed. A transaction may also be **Excluded** if you find that it does not belong in the accounting records at all. This may be a bank error or duplicate transaction

It short, you still have to pay attention! There is no autopilot. But using these features will save you lots of time once you get the hang of it.

*Working with **Bank transactions** does not move any actual money to and from your accounts at the bank.*

The Banking transactions review process is only telling QBO what has happened in the bank account.

C. THE RECEIPTS TAB

As I explained in Chapter 9, QuickBooks now allows you to upload or email a receipt to your system and then match it to an entry. This is a wonderful way to keep track of credit card receipts and make pulling documentation for auditors easy. In the Banking screen, select the third tab, **Receipts.**

You can scan a receipt and upload or email the receipt to receipts@quickbooks.com using your registered email (see **Manage Senders** for options) or use the mobile up to take a picture of the receipt to upload. The receipts will be listed below under the **For review** tab.

Click on the receipt to enter additional details as seen on the next page. The system will fill in the details it can from the scan. Correct or complete the details and choose *Save and Next*. QBO looks for a matching transaction and offers to post it or tells you No matches found.

If no match was found, choose *Create Expense* and an Expenditure will be posted in your system. When the related credit card or bank charge is downloaded, it will be matched to this receipt.

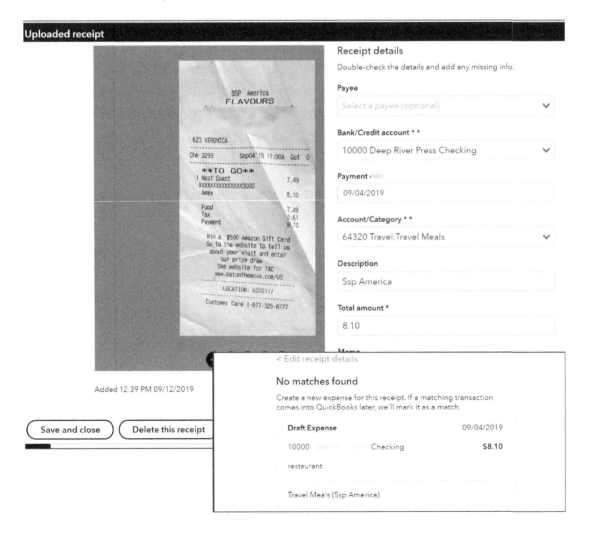

D. PREPARING FOR THE BANK RECONCILIATION

Now it is time to reconcile the bank accounts. However, rarely is there a month with only donation receipts and normal bill paying. You may have transferred cash between accounts, received an insufficient funds check from a donor, or voided a check you had written. All these will affect your bank reconciliation. I am going to walk you through a few things to do before you start the reconciliation process.

1. Internal Controls and Bank Reconciliations

The bank statements should be received and opened by someone besides the bookkeeper. This person should review the checks paid or money drafted and question any payments made to the bookkeeper or to an unknown vendor. If the bank does not send copies of the scanned checks, the reviewer should have access to the online banking program to view the checks. Paying fake vendors is a very common way to steal money, so any unusual or double payments should be investigated immediately. After verifying accuracy of the payments, the reviewer should initial the statement and give it to the bookkeeper to reconcile. The reconciliation should never be performed by anyone who has access to the cash.

2. Cash Transfers

Most organizations have a separate investment account from the checking account. If you deposit all donations into the checking account, you will want to transfer any excess cash into the investment account. When you need the funds, you will then transfer the appropriate amount from the investment account back into the checking.

There are two ways this is usually done. A check may be written from one account and deposited into the second account. Or the transfer is made through the bank or investment company's website or customer service associate. I'll show you how to record each of these ways in QBO.

3. Transfers without Writing a Check

In this first example, we will assume the money has been transferred online. Select *+New, Other, Transfer*.

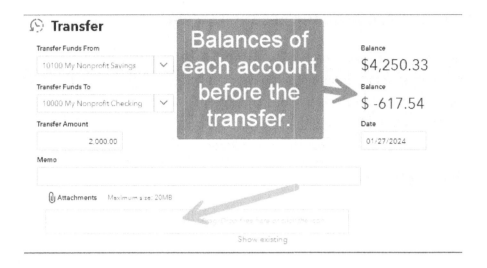

In the **Transfer Funds From** box, select from the drop-down menu the account the money was taken from. The system will show you the book balance before the transfer. Next, in the **Transfer Funds To** box, select the account the money was transferred to. Enter the **Transfer Amount** and the **Date**. In the **Memo** area, key in the reason for the transfer. If there is a supporting document you would like to have associated with this transfer, attach the file as I showed you in the previous chapter. Select *Save and close,* and your transfer has been recorded. You can also set up a recurring transfer by selecting *Make Recurring* at the bottom of the screen.

 At the time of this printing, you cannot assign a class to bank transfers. If you need this option, use the transfer cash via check option below.

4. **Transfer Cash via Check**

If you transfer cash between accounts by physically writing a check, you will take a different approach. This method also allows you to assign classes to your transfer transactions. Go to *+New, Vendor, Check.*

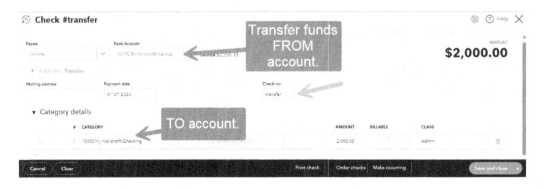

For the **Payee**, you will need to set up a vendor called Transfer. From the payee drop-down menu, type *Transfer* and click *Add Transfer*. Then, select *Details* to access the **Vendor Information** screen.

The **Display name as** *Transfers* shows up. The small box next to **Use display name** must be unchecked. Key in your organization's name in the **Print on check as** box. The other items can be left blank. Select *Save* to return to the **Check Transfer** screen (previous page).

In the **Bank Account** field, choose the account you are writing the check or transferring the money from. Now go to the bottom under **Category details**. Enter the amount of the transfer. Even though we usually select an expense account here, the drop-down menu includes the complete chart of accounts. Select the cash/bank or investment account this check will be deposited *to*, enter the related **Class,** and *Save & close*.

When you physically deposit this check, put it on a separate deposit slip. Recall that your other receipts go through Undeposited Funds and are therefore grouped together by deposit record. This transaction will not be included in the undeposited funds but will show up in the bank reconciliation on its own.

5. **Returned Checks**

Every so often you may have a check returned by the bank because a donor did not have sufficient funds in his account. You will need to take this out of the checking account in the system, record the bank fee for processing the bounced check, and invoice the donor for the original amount plus the fee.

In this example, the $50 check Ms. White wrote for dues was returned for non-sufficient funds. First, you will create an invoice to charge Ms. White for the returned check amount and the returned check fee. Go to *+New, Customers, Invoice (Pledge)*. Under the **Product/ Service** field, use the drop-down menu to create an item called "Returned Check". You can add the bank name if you use several bank accounts.

Because the item is tied directly to the bank account, you will need to create a returned check item. In the **Product/Service** details, choose your *Bank Account* instead of an **Income account**. *Save and close* when complete, and you will be back to the invoice.

The first item of the invoice is the "Returned Check" for the exact amount of the original check, and the second line is the returned check fee. The class for the Bank Charges will be your General or Admin account. The class for the Returned check can be left blank or set to Without Donor Restrictions. DO NOT charge it to your Program class. You can *Print* and mail with a cover letter or *Save and send* to email this invoice to the donor email on record.

Follow the regular Receive Payment step as discussed in Chapter 8 when the payment for the returned check is received.

6. **Voiding a Check**

There will be times that you need to void a lost check, or one made out for the wrong amount. Luckily, QBO makes this easy as you can void in the **Check** screen. *Search* using the magnifying glass icon on any screen.

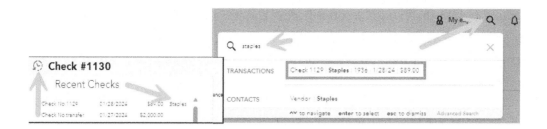

When you click inside the **Search box**, a list of the most recent transactions appears for the item you searched for. You can scroll down it or type in the check number, vendor name, or other identifying data to narrow the options. You can also select from recent checks form going to +*New, Vendor, Check,* and click on the clock icon.

Double click on the check you wish to void to bring up the **Check or Bill Payment** screen.

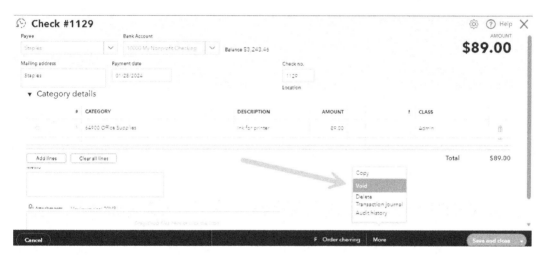

Select *Void* from the **More** menu found at the bottom of the check screen. Never use the **Delete** option as it does not leave an audit trail.

When you void the check, it records the check number in the system with an amount of $0, so there is an audit trail. After the check is voided, the screen reappears with **Void** in large letters at the upper right-hand side and the amount as $0.

If the check had been paid on an invoice, the invoice will now show as an open account payable. A new check can be printed to replace the voided one from the **Pay Bills** menu. If the bill was entered incorrectly, double click on the bill line item and edit it before reprinting the check. If you do not need to reissue the check, you will need to void the original invoice as discussed in Chapter 9.

To make certain the vendor account is now correct, select *Expenses, Vendors* from the side menu and scroll down to see the vendor whose check you just voided. For our example, the vendor detail for Staples is showing the amount for check #1129 as $0 since it was voided.

 The system allows you to enter transactions directly into the check register, but I would like to discourage you from doing so. You will get more accurate and detailed reports by entering your data through the transaction screens.

E. RECONCILING THE BANK ACCOUNT

Time to balance your checkbook, which QBO calls **Reconcile**. First, I would like you to make certain the system has recorded all of the money from undeposited funds into the checking account. Go to *+New, Other, Bank Deposit.*

Make sure you have submitted all of the deposits in the system. Once all of the deposits are made, you can begin reconciling.

 Check this screen each month before you begin reconciling to assure all deposits are recorded. It will save time during the reconciliation.

Next, go to **Bank transactions** and match or categorize any items from the bank feed or look at your bank statement for any automatic drafts or other charges. Compare those to the check register to see if all of them were entered. If not, go ahead and enter the missing charges through the **Vendor, Check** screen as we discussed in Chapter 9.

From the *Gear* icon, select *TOOLS, Reconcile.*

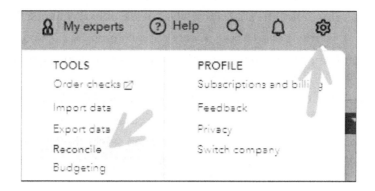

This will take you to the **Reconcile** screen at **Bank Transactions**. Choose the appropriate account from the drop-down arrow. If you are using subaccounts under checking, reconcile only the parent account. You can use this screen to reconcile any balance sheet account.

From your bank statement, you will need to enter the **Statement Ending Date** and **Ending Balance**. Make sure you have the ending date correct or your reconciliation will be more difficult.

The next screen will show you the **Statement Ending Balance** and the **Cleared Balance** as well as any **Difference**.

The next row has three buttons that allow you to see only **Payments, Deposits,** or **All** transactions for that time period. You can sort each column by clicking on the column title. This is helpful when looking for a particular amount or check number.

Now it's time to compare transactions you've entered into QBO to the bank statement. As you scroll down the list, you can select the small circle in the far-right corner for each of the transactions that has cleared the bank. You can select the top circle to select all of the transactions and then unclick any that have not yet cleared.

If your bank statement has a transaction that is not showing in QuickBooks, it could have been entered with the wrong date. To see transactions with dates outside of the statement date, select **View all** (to the left of the **Payments** button).

As you select transactions, the **Difference** amount changes. If it has not gotten to $0 once you have reviewed the transactions, you want to determine if it is a problem with the money going out or coming in. Under **Cleared Balance** are two categories, **Payments** and **Deposits**. The dollars in each of these should match the total payments and total deposits on your bank statement respectively. If the total deposit amount is lower than the statement, you are missing a deposit in QBO (or at least on the bank reconciliation).

If you see a payment that has not been entered, click **Save for later** at the top right and go to the appropriate transaction screen to enter. Once the change has been saved on the payments or checks screen, return to the reconciliation. The revised amount will appear. If it does not appear, go back and make certain you entered the correct date on the payment.

If you notice a check in your system was entered with the wrong amount, you can click on it within the reconciliation screen. The transaction screen will appear with the check data. Simply edit the amount and save. A warning may pop up. Select Yes and you will be back to the reconciliation screen.

The deposits listed on the bank statement should match those in your system due to using the Undeposited Funds option. If there is a receipt in the bank but not in your account, research the posting and record it on your side. If it is recorded on your books but not the bank, double check to be certain the receipt was not entered twice or entered with the wrong date. Otherwise, you will need to track down the missing deposit.

The **Edit info** button at the top allows you to change the ending balance and the ending date in case you entered them incorrectly when you started the process.

Another possible reconciliation error relates to the beginning balance. When you first bring up the reconcile screen, the system shows you the beginning balance, but does not allow you to adjust it. The system has calculated the beginning balance based on the previously cleared entries in the cash account.

If the beginning balance does not match the bank statement's beginning balance, someone has probably voided, deleted, or changed a transaction that was cleared in an earlier reconciliation.

For example, you pay Joe Smith $50 a week to mow the grass. He typically deposits the check the next day, and when you reconcile the bank account, you clear his checks. But one day he comes to you and says that he has lost last week's check. You void the check and issue him a new one. The only problem is you accidentally voided a check from last month that had already cleared. This will make your beginning balance not agree with the last reconciliation.

Luckily, the **Reconciliation History & Reports** will show any changes in the bank reconciliation since the last report. Go to the *Gear icon, Reconcile,* and look along the top of the screen.

Summary will bring up the reconciliation report for you to save as a PDF file. The **History by Account** will list all reconciliations previously done for this account, including any changes and auto adjustments.

If there have been any changes in a reconciliation, the amount of that change will appear in the list of reports in the Changes column. Simply click that line to see the details and then select the item that needs to be corrected and edit. Now go back to your reconciliation. Once you have matched everything possible with the bank statement, the bottom of the reconciliation screen should show a difference of $0. If there is a balance, you may have made an error in one of your transactions. Check for transpositions (if the difference is divisible by 9, it may mean you switched two numbers around—45 instead of 54) as well as differences between the check amounts recorded by the bank and in the accounting system. If nothing works, a last resort is to select *Finish Now*. The system will offer to allow you to record an **Auto Adjustment**.

 Only do this for small amounts after all other options have been exhausted. What looks like a small variance could be two large mistakes that happen to offset each other.

F. CREDIT CARD RECONCILIATION

QBO allows you to reconcile your credit cards the same way you reconcile the bank account. First connect your credit card to download charges from the credit card company via Bank transactions. This is a much easier way of getting all the individual charges into the system instead of keying them manually. Just like the bank accounts, you can set rules, so QBO will automatically match the expense to the correct general ledger account. Be sure to add the appropriate class!

 QBO will download the charges, but you need to be sure you have the receipts for each one. I recommend requiring each card holder to fill out a detailed expense report for his portion of the monthly credit card statement with the receipts and purpose attached.

A supervisor should review the expense reports and receipts and approve before the bookkeeper matches the downloaded transactions into the system.

Once all the transactions are approved and matched, they can be posted to the accounts. Simply go to *Gear, Tools, Reconcile* and change the account to the credit card account. Now reconcile the account just as you did with the bank.

G. RECONCILING PETTY CASH

Many organizations find it necessary to keep a petty cash account. These can take different forms; it may be a couple hundred dollars locked in a drawer, or gift cards purchased from local businesses that are used as needed.

Your organization should have written procedures and guidelines regarding the use of petty cash. One person should be responsible for maintaining the cash or cards. Receipts must be brought back to the bookkeeper in the amount of the cash expended. The fund is replenished with those receipts as the support.

I'll walk you through a typical example. Betty, the receptionist at your organization, has asked for a $200 petty cash fund. She promises to keep it in a security box locked in a filing cabinet behind her desk. People are always asking her to get donuts and coffee or office supplies at the last minute, and she doesn't personally have the funds to cover them until she can be reimbursed.

You will write a check made out to **Your Organization** to be cashed at your bank. Instead of an expense account number, you will set up a petty cash account with type marked as **Bank**. If you look at the account after you write the check, it will show a $200 balance.

At the end of the month, Betty brings you $175 of receipts and asks if she can get more money. First, verify that she has $25 of cash left. Betty should always have a combination of receipts and cash that equals $200. You will write a check for $175 and file the check voucher with the $175 of receipts under a Petty Cash file. From the +*New*, *Vendors*, *Check* screen, record the receipts under the **Expense** tab. Office supplies, meeting expenses, or whatever expense the receipts are for will be the expense accounts charged.

If you have purchased gift cards or prepaid credit cards, set up an account called Gift Cards with an account type of Prepaid Expenses. Each month, you should verify that the receipts and the balance of the gift cards equal the amount of the card purchases.

Consider checking the balance of the petty cash and receipts at irregular intervals during the month. This discourages people from thinking they can borrow money they may not be able to replace at month's end.

Summary

In this chapter, you learned how to handle transactions with financial institutions including how to:

- Understand the **Bank transaction** options
- Connect your accounts and set up bank rules
- Post feed transactions and import receipts to a match to transactions
- Prepare the bank reconciliation
- Handle cash transfers and record returned and voided checks
- Find errors in the reconciliation
- Reconcile the credit cards and petty cash

Now that you've entered all the transactions and reconciled your accounts for the month, it's time to run reports. On to Chapter 12 to learn what reports are available and what information you need to most effectively show the financial status of your organization.

12

WHERE DO WE STAND?
—DESIGNING & RUNNING REPORTS

As you were working through this book, you may have been asking yourself, "Why do I have to track the finances in such detail?" Being able to access accurate financial reports is crucial to funding the nonprofit's mission. Every entry helps paint a fuller picture for current and future donors of how well your organization is serving out its mission. In this chapter, I will explain the different types of reports specific to an organization needs, walk you through the standard QuickBooks options, and show you how to design and export customized reports.

A. TYPES OF REPORTS

At a minimum, all organizations need two basic reports—the **Balance Sheet** and the **Income Statement (or Profit and Loss Statement)**. Nonprofits call these reports **Statement of Financial Position** and **Statement of Activities**. The Balance Sheet (or Statement of Financial Position) is a snapshot of what the organization owns, owes, and what is left in net assets as of a certain date. The Income Statement (or Statement of Activities) summarizes the revenues and expenses over a defined period.

This sounds like accountant talk again, doesn't it? I'm afraid you will have to humor me a bit to assure you are comfortable with the differences and will know when to run which report. The balance sheet indicates the financial health of your organization. If assets are greater than liabilities, you own more than you owe. What is left is the net assets. Net assets are the accumulated amount of the difference between the amount owned versus owed since the organization's inception.

The income statement reflects the operations of your organization. If you want to know how much money has been donated to your organization this year and what expenses have been incurred, you would run an income statement report for the year. If you need to know how much was donated in the last quarter, you could run the report for a three-month period.

Besides the two primary reports, you would probably like to see who your biggest donors are, who has donated how much, how your donations and expenses compare to your budgets, how much money is expected from dues, and how much you owe vendors. QBO allows you to run reports on all of this information and more. Let's walk through how to navigate the reports and see what options you have.

B. NAVIGATING THE REPORTS CENTER

Reports are very easy to access in QBO. Go to the left *Menu, Reports.*

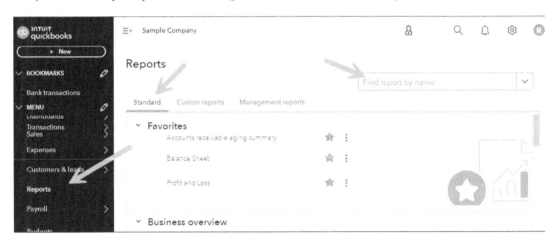

You can find a report by searching for its name in the **Find report by name** box. Below that box there are three headings: **Standard, Custom Reports,** and **Management Reports**. QBO saves your specific reports to these various tabs. Think of these headings as file folders to help you organize your reports and get to the ones you need quickly.

The **Standard Reports** tab has several subsets that you can expand or condense by selecting the side arrow. The **Favorites** section is populated by the reports you run the most often. You can select these by finding reports in the other areas clicking the **star** icon next to the report name. The others are categories by types of reports, i.e. **Who owes you, What you owe**, etc. Take some time to look around these sections to see what is available.

Custom Reports stores the reports you have customized and saved. This saves you from having to reenter the parameters on a report the next time you wish to run it. **Management Reports** are the groupings of reports. If you prepare a board package each month, this is the area you could store the grouping.

The nice thing about QBO is that the way you set parameters and formats stays consistent across all reports. Let's go over the options.

C. DEFINING THE PARAMETERS AND SAVING CUSTOMIZATIONS

From the **Reports** screen, select the *Standard* tab, *Favorites* section. Look for *Statement of Activities* or *Profit and Loss Statement*.

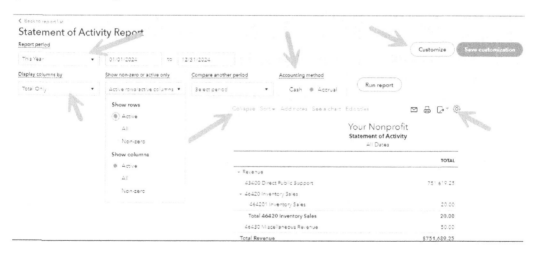

A wonderful feature of QBO reports is the ability to do quite a bit of customization on the initial screen. You can set the **Report period** with last month, this year to last month, and many more including a range of date you select. For example, you may want to see information for a specific month, quarter, or the entire year. Simply change the beginning and ending dates and select *Run Report* to refresh.

Display columns by is usually Total Only, but you can also choose, Days, Weeks, Months, Quarters, Donors, Vendors, Classes, etc. The **Show non-zero or active only** allows you to suppress columns or rows with $0 to simplify reports. If you would like to **Compare another period**, the drop-down arrow offers options for Previous Period, Previous Period, Year to Date, as well as Percent of Row, Column, Income, or Expense.

The **Accounting Method** determines whether this report will be calculated on a **Cash Basis** or **Accrual**. The reports will default to whichever method you chose back in the Your Company, Account and Settings. Recalling our earlier chapters, the cash basis option will display only transactions for which cash has been received or paid out. If you have recorded dues receivable for the year but want to run a profit and loss based on the dues actually received, select the *Cash* basis. The accrual option will display transactions based on the invoice date, not when cash was exchanged.

The next line has a **Collapse** option. Report data can be "rolled up" or totaled into parent accounts. This is where the careful thought you put into the chart of accounts shows. If the report is already *collapsed*, the button will say **Expand**. Selecting *Expand* will cause the report to show each sub-account. You can click on the parent accounts individually so your report will show the details of some parents and only the summary of others. **Sort** allows you to display the report with ascending or descending amounts. This is handy if you want a report to show the largest expenses or revenues first. **Add notes** allows you to type in explanations to be saved with the report.

To the right on that line are icons for **Email, Print, Export**, and a **Gear** to condense the lines to make the report more compact and, in some reports, exclude certain columns or reorder them. The **Export** icon allows you to send the report to an Excel spreadsheet, save it as a PDF, or add it to the **Management Reports** on the Report home screen. The above options make it easy to see most of the data you may need from standard reports, but you will wish to run more specific reports from time to time. That is when you will want to select the **Customize** button near the upper right corner.

Let's play around with the **Customize** options and learn how to make some changes to reports. Select *Customize* to see the four sections of options: **General, Rows/Columns, Filter,** and **Header/Footer.** Because these are so important, we will talk about each section individually.

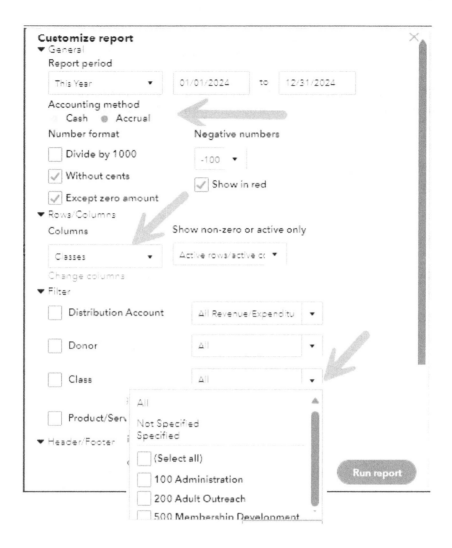

Under the **General** section, you can change the time period and accounting method as mentioned on the main page.

Number format and **Negative numbers** give you options to format and display amounts. The **Number format** area allows you to produce reports with the numbers rounded by 1000, without the cents showing, or omitting zero balances. Unless you are a very large organization, I doubt you'll need to round by 1000. The **Negative numbers** options let you decide if negatives should be shown with a minus sign, parentheses, a trailing minus sign, or in bright red. To save ink costs for printed reports, I'd recommend staying away from the colors.

Next the **Rows/Columns** section allows you to decide what columns you would like to see on the report. For example, you may want to run a report with Classes in the columns. You can also select **Change columns** compare to previous periods and show percentage. This can also be done on the **Display columns** line on the main report page.

The next section is **Filter. Lists** provides drop-down menus that allow you to filter reports if you want to display information for a specific **Donor, Vendor, Product/Service,** or **Class**. This is very useful for grant (**Donor**) or program (**Class**) reporting.

Header/Footer is where you will label your report. It will default to the company name and report title, but you can type anything in the open boxes.

If you don't want some of this information to show on the report, simply unselect the box to the left of the choice.

Now you can select *Run Report* and you will see a Profit and Loss report. If you click on **Collapse**, the system will hide subaccounts and display totals by parent account. This is very handy to review for errors. Note the **Accrual Basis** in the upper right corner. If you wanted a cash basis report, simply press the circle by *Cash*.

Once you have the report looking the way you'd like, press *Save Customization*.

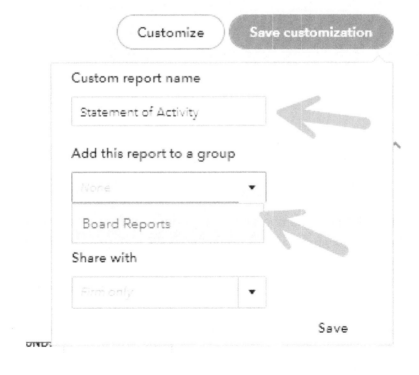

You may now give the report a custom name. You may group reports together and send a single email by setting up a new group. **Add this to a group** and choose whether to share with others or not. Select *Save* and you will be taken back to the report. In the upper left corner, select *Back to report list* and click on the *Custom reports* tab. You will now see the Group and your custom report.

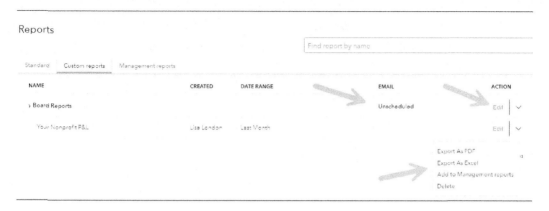

The drop down arrow on the right side of the screen will give you options to **Export** the reports. If you want your reports to be emailed automatically on a set day each month, you can **Edit** the Group level.

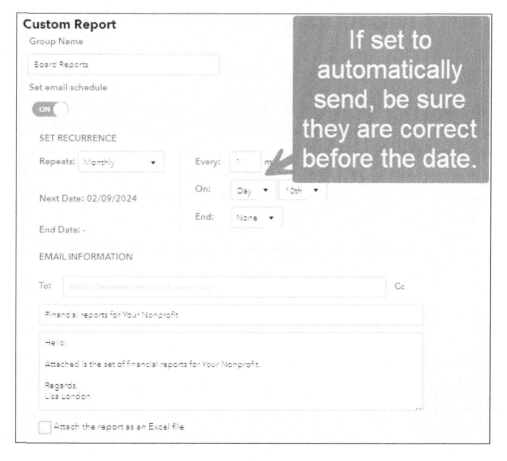

I would warn you to be very careful when setting up automatic emails. Make sure you set up processes for you to review the financial statements before they are sent.

Click the **X** in the top right corner to get back to the report list. Select the report name to bring the financial statement back up. You can see the details for any line item by clicking on the amount. Any field that turns blue when you hover over it can be clicked on to see the details.

 *I'll be referring to the ability to link to the transactions from reports as **drilling down**. In later chapters, if I tell you to drill down on a report, I mean click on the transaction in question.*

I clicked account **Books, Subscriptions, Reference**.

Filters: Distribution Account ✕

Sort ▾ Add notes

Your Nonprofit
Transaction Report
All Dates

Click to be taken to entry screen.

DATE	TRANSACTION TYPE	ADJ	NAME	ACCOUNT	SPLIT	AMOUNT	BALANCE
▾ Books, Subscriptions, Reference							
10/09/2019	Check	No	Getrude Park	65010 Books, Subsc	10100 Cash & Invest Checking A...	250.00	250.00
10/09/2019	Expenditure	No	Book Supply	65010 Books, Subsc	20300 Credit Card		250.00
10/10/2019	Vendor Credit	No	Book Supply	65010 Books, Subsc	20000 Accounts Payable	-5.95	244.05
Total for Books, Subscriptions, Reference						$244.05	
TOTAL						$244.05	

You can continue to click or "drill down" any of these amounts in this **Transaction Report** to be taken to the original transaction screen. That means you will be taken to the sales receipt, invoice, check, or expense screen where you entered the transaction. If there is an error, it can be fixed and saved. The system will alert you that the report needs to be refreshed. Select the *Run Report* button on the top menu, and the report will show the most up-to-date information.

Though QBO has numerous types of reports, you will navigate around them and change the parameters in the same way.

D. MOST USEFUL REPORTS

Go back to the **Reports** screen and review what types of reports are available under each of the categories. You can also search for reports by keying the name into the **Find report by name** search box.

I'll explain some of the reports you are most likely to need. The **Report Name** column also includes some of the customization steps needed. Play around with these reports and see what your information your organization can use.

There are reports related to the tax filings required for nonprofits (IRS Form 990). As of the writing of this book, QBO has reporting limitations. It cannot produce a report specific enough for the 990. There are work arounds to design a report that contains the information needed to complete the 990. A QBO ProAdvisor or other accounting professional may be able to assist you with this.

We looked at an overall Profit and Loss statement earlier, but now, let's walk through the selections for **Profit and Loss by Class (or Statement of Activities by Class)** to show you how to customize your own reports. We will use this report as it will give information by each of the programs. First, search and run the **Statement of Activities by Class** report. Use the search box and start typing the keywords to get a list.

I want to see	Report Name	Description
Biggest Donors/ Grants	Go to: Sales and customers section, Sales by Donor Summary, then *Customize, Filter, Product/ Services, Donations.* Finally, *Sort* total in descending order.	Lists donors/members in order of donation size.
Donor Contribution Summary	Go to: Sales and customers section, Sales by Donor Summary, then *Customize, Filter, Product/ Services,* select appropriate *Donations* items.	Lists donations subtotaled by donors. Use this list to develop year-end giving statements.
Programs/Projects Report	Go to: Business overview, Profit and Loss by Class, then *Customize, Filter, Class,* choose class or classes of your choice	Details income and expenses for an individual program.
Statement of Activities	Profit and Loss	Details income and expenses for the organization in total.
Statement of Financial Position	Balance Sheet or Balance Sheet Summary	Shows amount owned, owed, and Net Assets.

When the report opens, you can click the title and subtitle and change the name of the report from **Statement of Activities by Class** to **Statement of Activities by Program**.

As we learned earlier, you can change the date range, header, etc. by using the buttons across the top of this screen. The **Collapse** button will hide the detail accounts. Additionally, you can change the size of the columns by hovering your mouse over the little downward arrow between the columns. When the cursor changes to a **+**, slide it to the left to make the column narrower or to the right to make it wider.

Looking across the columns, you see each program that was set up as a class. For each program, you can scan down the reports to see the income, operating expenses, and a net operating income line. This tells you how much you have received from regular donations and grants and the related expenses. Below the **Net Operating Income** line are the non-operating income and expenses. These are the out-of-the-ordinary expenses or revenues that may occur at your organization.

This report can be customized to show only one or some of the programs by using the **Customize** button and selecting *Filter, Classes*. If you have lots of classes, each will be in a different column, and the print would be very difficult to read.

E. EXPORTING REPORTS TO A SPREADSHEET

I just want to warn you, this section assumes you know Excel well enough to do basic formulas, adding worksheets, and formatting. As an accountant, I'm afraid I assume everyone uses Excel as much as I do. But if you are not familiar with the spreadsheet program, you may wish to ask for help from someone who is as you go through this section.

Once you have pulled up the report you'd like to export, select *Export, Excel (XLSX) or Excel (XLS)* from the top of the report screen. Excel XLSX is a newer format than XLS; but, newer versions of Microsoft Excel open both formats, which have the same basic functionality. Beyond that I will have to direct you to Google or the Microsoft website to learn more and decide which format works best for you.

The new spreadsheet downloads immediately. Look for it at the top of your browser screen or in the **Downloads** file.

	A	E	F	G	H	I	J	K	L	M	N	O
1						We Care Community Foundation						
2						Profit & Loss by Class						
3						January - December 2020						
4												
5		Total 200 ED	221 Teacher Ed	500 M&G	511 Managemen t	Total 500 M&G	521 Governanc e	531 Membersh ip developm ent	600 S/E	611 Annual Dinner	Total 600 S/E	621 Promotion - Annual Dinner
6	Income											
7	4 Contributed support	0.00				0.00					0.00	
8	4010 Indiv/business contributi	0.00				0.00					0.00	
9	4110 Donated pro services - G	0.00	5,000.00		1,200.00	1,200.00					0.00	
10	4120 Donated other serv - non	0.00	0.00			0.00					0.00	
11	4130 Donated use of facilities	0.00	1,000.00			0.00					0.00	
12	4140 Gifts in kind - goods	0.00	15,000.00			0.00					0.00	
13	4210 Corporate/business gran	0.00	25,000.00			0.00					0.00	15,000.00
14	4230 Foundation/trust grants	0.00				0.00					0.00	
15	4520 Federal grants	0.00				0.00					0.00	
16	4540 Local government grants	0.00	150,000.00			0.00					0.00	
17	Total 4 Contributed support	$ 0.00	$196,000.00	$ 0.00	$ 1,200.00	$ 1,200.00	$ 0.00	$ 0.00	$ 0.00	$ 0.00	$ 0.00	$ 15,000.00
18	5 Earned revenues	0.00				0.00					0.00	
19	5180 Program service fees	20,000.00				0.00					0.00	
20	5210 Membership dues - indiv	0.00				0.00		96,250.00			0.00	
21	5310 Interest-savings/short-te	0.00			14,076.55	14,076.55					0.00	
22	5440 Gross sales - invenotry	0.00	1,100.00			0.00					0.00	
23	Total 5 Earned revenues	$ 20,000.00	$ 1,100.00	$ 0.00	$ 14,076.55	$ 14,076.55	$ 0.00	$96,250.00	$ 0.00	$ 0.00	$ 0.00	$ 0.00
24	5800 Special events	0.00				0.00					0.00	

Profit & Loss by Class

This worksheet has all of the data from the QBO report. If you would like this report to only show the top-level (parent) accounts, you would **Collapse** the report before exporting to Excel.

Once you are in the spreadsheet, you can save space by rounding to the nearest whole dollar instead of showing the cents. To do this, highlight the entire Excel worksheet and click on the small arrow pointing to the right twice to remove any numbers after the decimal.

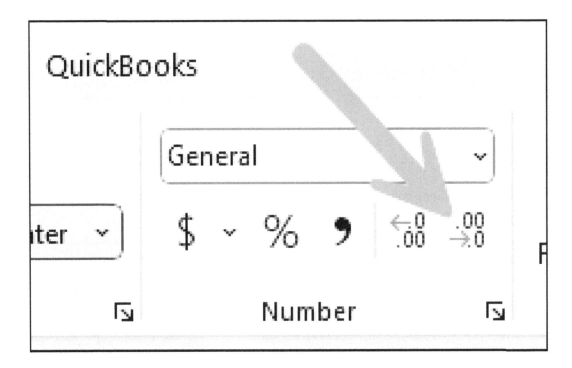

You are ready to reduce the columns to the narrowest size possible while keeping the numbers legible. Holding your cursor at the line between spreadsheet columns will change it to a bold **+**. You can then move the edge of the column to the right or left. Do this for each of the columns until you are happy with the result.

You can also add headings, logos, change the fonts, etc. to make the report look exactly like you want. Save the spreadsheet and note the name and place.

All reports in QBO can be exported to a spreadsheet with your customized headings and formatting. Take a few minutes and try some other reports with the sample company. Also, use the spreadsheet program to change the fonts and practice exporting. You will find this a handy tool.

You may also notice another tab in your Excel sheet called **QuickBooks**. This is an advanced feature that lets you set up QuickBooks reports and then have them updated. I won't be covering it in this book, but once you get familiar with the system, try it out using the **Help** function.

F. OTHER MISCELLANEOUS REPORTS

1. Dues Receivable, & Donor Information

There are several other reports you will want to keep an eye on. If you have entered dues or pledges as invoices, you can search for and run the **Accounts Receivable Aging Summary** report. This report lists the donors and what amount owed is still outstanding.

Choose today's date and you will see how much is owed to your organization as of today. The **Accounts Receivable Aging Detail** is the same report but lists the individual invoices entered by donor.

Search and run the **Customer or Donor Contact List** which can be printed, emailed, exported to Excel, or printed to PDF format. Use the **Gear** icon next to the Export icon to eliminate or reorder the columns. The Excel file can also be imported into other software. To print mailing labels, you will need to export the customer list and upload it to another program like Microsoft Word.

2. Accounts Payable & Vendor Information

If you have been entering your bills as they are received, but not yet paid, you can search for the **Accounts Payable Aging Summary** report. This is the accounts payable report which shows all the bills that have been entered but not yet paid and when they are due. It is a useful tool for cash-flow management. Search for the **Transaction List by Vendor** to run reports on all transactions for a particular vendor.

3. Deposit Detail

Search for the **Deposit Detail** report to view every deposit made and the bank account it went to along with the individual transactions that made up the deposit. If the deposits on your bank account do not tie to the deposits listed in your accounts during your bank reconciliation, refer to this report to see if you put the money in the wrong account in QBO.

Summary

Having accurate and easily accessible reports is the hallmark of a good accounting system. In this chapter you learned how to:

- Understand the types of reports available in QBO
- Navigate the reports center
- Customize reports
- Group reports to be emailed together
- Find the most useful reports
- Export reports to a spreadsheet
- Utilize other miscellaneous reports

The final section of the reports is **Budgets.** In the next chapter, I'll show you how to input your budgets and best utilize this powerful tool.

13

AM I MEETING MY TARGETS? BUDGETING

Planning for the future is crucial for any nonprofit. Preparing an annual budget requires an organization to consider their priorities. Because there is a limit to the donations expected to be received, there is also a limit to the services that can be offered.

 Approach the budgeting process as a way to get consensus around the priorities of your organization.

A. THE BUDGET PROCESS

Budgets are typically done on operating income and expenses. Income and expenses outside of normal organization operations (non-operating income and expenses, like the receipt of a bequest or repaving the parking lot) only need to be budgeted if they are substantial.

The budget process will have several steps. First you must consider if you need budgets at a top level (total organization only) or program by program. Budgeting at the program level will take more time but will also give you more information.

You may also wish to budget by grant. QBO allows you to input class (program) budgets separate from the whole organization budget. If you prepare program budgets for all areas (including administration), this will summarize to a total organizational budget.

To begin budgeting, you need to determine what donations and other revenues can be reasonably expected. If your membership and donations have been consistent over the years, you can use historical trends and tweak them for any likely changes.

For example, if pledges have consistently been close to $100,000 for the last five years, you are probably safe budgeting $100,000 for next year. But if a large donor moved to another state, consider reducing the expected dues by their usual donation.

Other donations are usually budgeted based on promises to give and historical rates. This would include money received from foundations, memorials, rent, etc. Investment income can be budgeted based on expected returns of the investments. If you have $100,000 in a money market account that is currently paying 2% interest, you would budget $2000 of investment income.

For the expense budgets, I like to get buy-in from the heads of the programs. Start by printing out a report showing each program director how much money they have spent this year.

Under Reports, search for the **Profit and Loss or Statement of Activities by Class** report and filter it for each class (You learned how to filter the reports in the last chapter). I like to make the date range the last twelve months, so they have their actual cost for a year. You may email the resulting report to directors directly from this screen and include in the email a request for budget submissions.

Next, ask your program heads to submit their budget proposal of expected needs, and if it is substantially different than this year, an explanation should be included. I refer to this as the wish list. Be sure to remind the directors it is not part of the budget until approved by the finance committee or governing board.

Preparing their proposal and explanation encourages the program directors to think about what they would like to do differently. The written documentation is a good resource for the governing board as they deliberate on how to divide the budget dollars. This also gives you the information to put in a class (program) budget in QBO.

Besides program expenses, your organization has facilities and other overhead expenditures. These can be calculated based on historical information or contracts. If you are allocating this expense across the programs, save yourself time by waiting until all of the direct program costs have been budgeted. Then you can do a one-time calculation to allocate the overhead based on percentage of space used, number of employees, or percentage of total costs.

For example, use a spreadsheet to estimate all of your building expenses. If you have three programs- Administration, Publications, and Education, you would add one third of the expected building expenses to each of these three budgets. You can do the same thing for salaries if you allocate people over more than one program. Some organizations use different allocation percentages for facilities costs versus supplies and administrative costs.

> *Consider exporting last year's actual overhead expenses to a spreadsheet. You can use formulas that add an inflation percentage and then allocate by program. The allocation would be input into QuickBooks' budget by account.*

B. ENTERING YOUR BUDGET

Once you have compiled all the information from the program directors, pledge cards, historical information, and anywhere else, it is time to put it all together in a budget. You will probably go through several iterations before your board decides on a final budget, so don't worry if you don't have all the information you would like.

It is very important that you are organized during the budget formation progress. Each line item should have an assigned class (program). The lines that don't have a specific program should be assigned to the Unrestricted class. The more organized you are, the easier budget entry will be.

There are two ways to access the **Budget** area. From the *Gear* icon, select *TOOLS*, *Budgeting* or go to the menu and select *Budgets*.

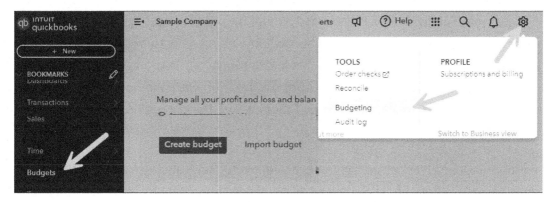

If you have never created a budget, QBO will walk you through the process. You can either create a budget from scratch or historical information you have already entered. Think of this step as creating a shell of a budget from which you can enter and adjust numbers. Before you begin, you will need to think about whether you will be preparing a top-level organizational budget only or program level budgets that will roll up to the top level.

There are two ways to set up a budget in QBO. You can create one the system takes you through or you can import a budget from an Excel worksheet. I'll take you through both processes.

To get started, select **Create budget.**

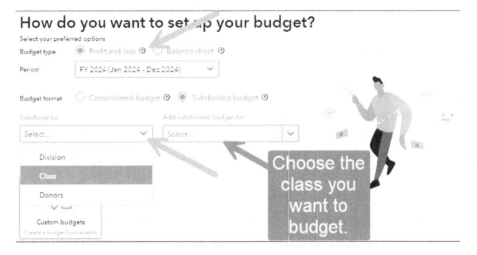

For the **Budget** type, select *Profit and loss*. This type of budget will track actual expenses to expected expenses. The Balance sheet budget is designed to help with cash flow.

Next select the period you are budgeting-the drop-down arrow will give you choices by fiscal year. **Subdivide by** allows you to budget by location, class, or even donors. The Class and Location options will only be available if you have turned on **Track classes** and **Track locations** in **Advanced Accounts and Settings** (see Chapter 2). **Don't subdivide** is used if you are budgeting for the entire organization with one budget. The **Classes** option is needed to create a budget by **Program.** The **Donors** option is used to create a budget by **Grant**.

For our purposes, let's set up the budget to allow for several classes. Select *Class* and then you can click on the arrow under **Add subdivided budget for** to select all the classes (or if you only want to budget for a few, select them individually).

This will open a data entry screen for the budget.

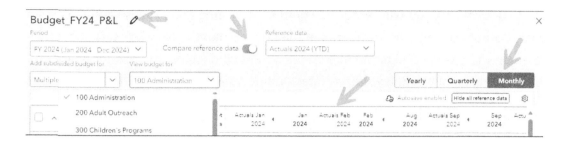

First you will need to edit the name of the budget using the pencil icon at the top. If you are doing several program budgets, figure out a naming protocol. If it is for the overall organization, perhaps *2025 Your Nonprofit Budget* is sufficient. If you will be adding budgets by class, consider *2025 Class Name Budget*.

The default **Fiscal Year** corresponds to your selections in the **My Company Account and settings** we reviewed in Chapter 2. The drop-down arrow will allow you to set up budgets for seven separate years. Select the year you wish to enter.

Compare reference data is a very handy option. It adds columns with actual data for each time period, so you can compare your expected budget and see if it needs to be adjusted based on historical patterns. The system also lets you decide which year you would like the actual data from.

QBO allows you to **Add subdivided budget for** Classes, Locations, or Donors. Because we had selected Classes when we first created the budget, we have the list of classes to choose which one we are budgeting for.

To the right are three boxes, **Yearly, Quarterly,** and **Monthly**. These are the intervals you can use for your budget. I highly recommend using a monthly budget. It is easier to see if you are on track or not for the year with interim information and to make adjustments as needed in your organization.

Whether you just created your budget from scratch or are viewing a budget that has already been entered, you will view, manage, and enter amounts for your budgets in the main budget entry screen. Let's take a look at it.

At the top of the Budgets screen, select the budget you are working on. You may have multiple budgets for the same year or budgets from previous years. Make sure they are clearly labeled so you don't get confused. Click in the *Name* box to change the name of the selected budget if necessary. Select the *Gear* icon to **Autosave budget**, simplify or expand your view and to **Hide empty rows** (accounts without budget amounts).

In the left column, you will recognize your list of income and expense accounts from your chart of accounts. Across the top of the grid are months. Now let's talk about how to enter and change budget numbers. First you need to select the row for which you are entering amounts. Below, I have selected line 43300 – Direct Public Grants.

The selected line is highlighted. If I key in $1000 in the **Budget Totals** box, QBO will spread the total amount over the 12 months evenly. If I go down to the next row and put $800 in **JAN** and hit *Enter*, the cursor moves to the next line item, leaving all of the other months in the row empty. But if I put an amount in February and click on the small blue arrow, it tells me I can **Click to copy the value across the row.** As you can see in the example above, you can select any month and have it copy for the rest of the year. You can also use the *Enter* key to change that month only.

The **TOTAL** is calculated for you to verify that it is the correct annual amount. When you are done entering lines of the budget, **Save**.

If you need to edit any of these entries, simply highlight the line the account is on and key over the incorrect data in the entry fields. Don't forget to *Save*.

I recommend taking the time to enter your budget by month, based on historical data and current information. You'll be able to report actual versus budgeted costs by month, allowing for more accurate information. If you need it for reporting purposes, you can create separate budgets entered by quarter or year.

To go back to your budget, go to *Gear, Tools, Budgeting*. This will bring up a list of all the budgets you have entered.

Run this report to check your data entry.

The upper right corner has a **Create budget** button that allows you to start a new budget. Click on the down arrow next to **Run Budget Overview report** to see several options. **View/Edit** brings the data entry screen back up, **Archive** takes the report off of your list (but doesn't delete it). **Duplicate** will make a copy of this budget. This is useful if the next year's budget will be similar to the current budget. **Delete** allows you to remove the budget completely-this is irreversible so be careful.

After you have entered your budget numbers, select **Run Budgets vs Actuals report** to print out and double check your data entry. It can also be accessed through the **Reports** menu under **Business Overview**.

After you are finished with the first budget, **Create budget** again to enter the next Class. Don't forget to keep to the same naming protocol.

The same process is used to create a budget subdivided by Donor (used for grants). The difference is that you can enter the budget by Account or Donor (grant).

C. IMPORTING BUDGETS

A new feature of QBO is to be able to import your budget from an Excel spreadsheet. As many of us tend to do the budgets in a spreadsheet before entering, this is a huge time saver. Go to *Menu, Budgets, Import budget.* A wizard will take you through the steps.

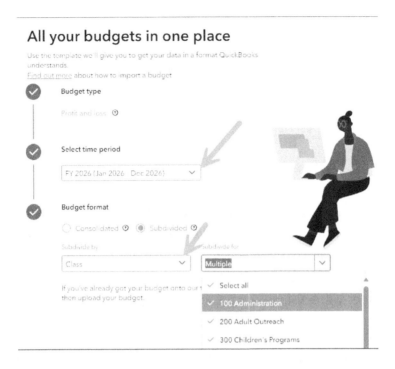

Select the year for the budget, choose **Consolidated** if you are doing a top line budget, **Subdivided** if you are entering by class. The next page offers a template-**USE IT!** Not only will it make sure your data is in the right format, it will prepopulate with your classes and accounts.

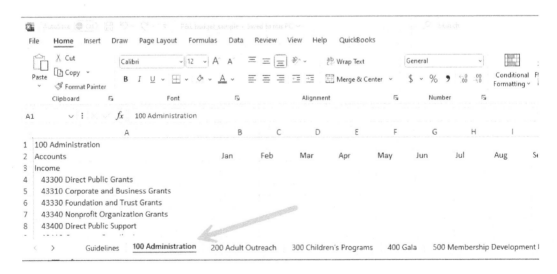

The Guidelines tab reminds you not to change the sheet names or row and column labels. Enter your budget by class and save the spreadsheet on your computer where you can find it.

Go back to the **Budget Import** screen.

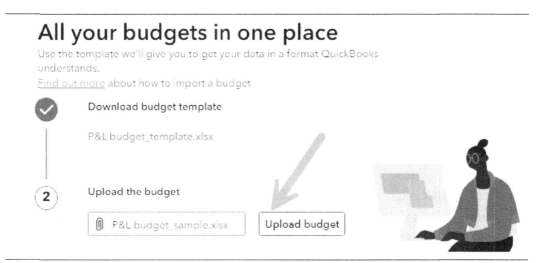

Click *Upload budget* and attach your spreadsheet. Click *Next* to continue. The system will let you know it is importing the data and once it is complete, you can view the budget. Edit anything as you did above when you entered the budget manually.

Next, we will look at how amounts entered into your budget will flow through to reports to provide useful information.

D. BUDGET REPORTS

Let's see what kind of reports we can generate once a budget is input. From the left **Menu**, select *Reports*. There are two main budget reports: **Budget Overview** and **Budget vs. Actuals**. The **Budget Overview** report shows a summary of budgeted amounts for a specific account. The **Budget vs. Actuals** report shows your budgeted income and expenses to the actual amounts so you can tell whether you are over or under budget.

First let's type *Budget Overview* in the **Search** box near the top of the screen. In the screen that opens, make sure that the correct budget is selected.

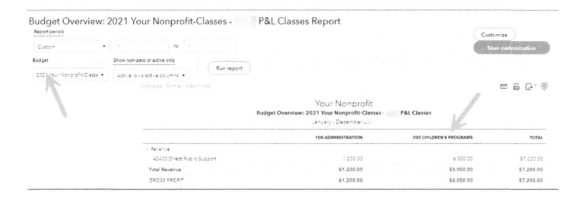

Double check that you have selected the correct **Budget**. Because I had selected a budget with multiple classes, the classes are listed across the top and totaled. This is a great way to double check your data entry.

Now, let's look at the **Budget vs. Actuals** report. In the upper left corner, select *Back to report list*. Use the **Search** box and find the **Budget vs. Actuals** report. Once the report window opens, make sure that the correct budget is selected.

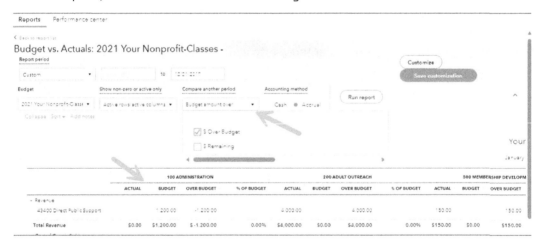

You may want the report to show **$ Over Budget, % of Budget, $ Remaining, or % Remaining**. Each of these adds another column, so the report can get very wide. You'll probably only want to use these when running a report on one class at a time.

To do that, select *Customize, Filter, Class*. Select the class you want and *Run report*. Use the main screen to then look at the **Budget amount over** options.

This is a report you will want to analyze each month. Comparing your actual revenues and expenses to budgets will help your organization track its financial goals. It shows how your programs' expenses are comparing to your expectations.

The **TOTAL** column gives you the variance for the entire organization. Filter the report to each of the individual programs and email a copy to the program director each month directly from QBO.

Save each program's budget by clicking *Save Customizations* and naming the report for that program. This will allow you to send reports to program directors without having to recreate the reports each time.

Experiment with the various budget reports. Change the parameters and see what is most useful for your organization. Export the reports to spreadsheets for further analysis or to make them more aesthetically pleasing.

Summary

I hope I have expressed the need for good budgeting. It is not only a tool to help you run your organization, but also a good control feature to stop mistakes and fraud. In this chapter you learned how to:

- Develop a budget process
- Enter your organization budget by month, quarter or year
- Enter budgets by programs or grants manually
- Import budgets
- Run and customize budget reports

We are rapidly approaching the end. Let's move on to the next chapter to see what needs to be done at the end of each month and year.

14

IT'S MONTH END &/OR YEAR END —WHAT NOW?

You have entered all your transactions and reconciled your bank account. Before you print out the financial statements for the treasurer or board, let's do a review of the data.

On the next page is a checklist of things to do each month and the additional requirements for year end. You may need to add a few other things for your specific organization, but this should get you started.

As you look down the list, you will see that we have covered almost everything except allocating the fund balances.

In the first chapter, I explained how QBO is designed for businesses which only have one equity account for net income: Retained Earnings. Your organization, however, has two different equity accounts: Net Assets without Donor Restrictions and Net Assets with Donor Restrictions.

Additionally, you may have funds you need to track that carry forward year after year and are never closed out. In this chapter, I'll show you how to develop the funds report and how to record your net income (or loss) into the correct net assets account.

A. MONTH AND YEAR-END CHECKLIST

Duties	Chapter	Completed
Enter all bills.	9	
Enter any vendor credits.	9	

Pay all bills.	9	
Enter any manual checks.	9	
Download all online banking payments.	9	
Download all bank drafts.	9	
Enter payroll.	10	
Pay any payroll liabilities.	10	
Enter any invoices required (including dues).	8	
Enter all donations.	8	
Enter any other receipts.	8	
Match credit card charges to receipts.	9/11	
Reconcile credit card bills.	11	
Reconcile bank account to statement.	11	
Charge prepaid expenses.	14	
Review Receivable Aging Report.	12	
Review Payable Aging Report.	12	
Review Statement of Financial Position (Balance Sheet).	12	
Review Statement of Activities by Class (P&L).	12	
Review P&L Comparison to Budget.	13	
*Allocate fund balances.	14	
*Set year-end closing date.	14	
* Electronically submit 1099s and 1096.	14	
* Electronically submit W-2s and W-3.	14	

B. REVIEWING YOUR TRANSACTIONS

The first step in closing the books for the month is to make certain everything has been accounted for correctly. To do that, let's start with the **Statement of Financial Position** (or Balance Sheet as it is known in the for-profit world). Go to *Reports, Reports* and search for *Balance Sheet* (or *Statement of Financial Position)*. Run the report with the month-end date you are closing. Be sure to select the *Accrual* option.

Make sure the report is expanded (you should see the **Collapse** button at the top). This report will list all the assets and liabilities for your organization. I like to print out a copy to make notes on. At the top are the cash accounts. Check your reconciliation summaries to see that each account ties to the reconciliation you performed. If you have a petty cash account, it should tie to the amount of cash in the drawer. Investments should tie to the brokerage reconciliations. If there are any differences, investigate and correct the errors or the reconciliations.

 On the main Reports screen, you can scroll down and see the list of reports available. Click the **Star** icon next to the reports you will be using each month. This will put them at the top of the page in the **Favorites** box.

Undeposited funds should only have a balance if a deposit has not been taken to the bank.

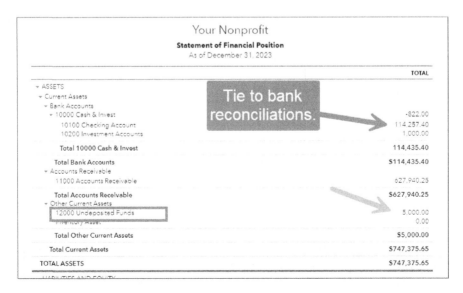

In this example, the undeposited funds account is showing a $5,000.00 balance, but we know the organization has made all the deposits. Let's drill down on the account and see what is left.

		Your Nonprofit					
		Transaction Report					
		All Dates					
DATE	**TRANSACTION TYPE**	**NAME**	**ACCOUNT**	**SPLIT**		**AMOUNT**	**BALANCE**
∨ Undeposited Funds							
09/30/20	Receipt	Aaron E Berhanu	12000 Undeposited F	43400 Direct Public Suppor		4,000.00	107,000.00
10/01/20	Deposit	HHS:Research Next Year	12000 Undeposited F	10100 Cash & Invest:Check..		-100,000.00	7,000.00
10/03/20	Deposit		12000 Undeposited F	10100 Cash & Invest:Check..		-3,000.00	4,000.00
10/03/20	Deposit		12000 Undeposited F	10100 Cash & Invest:Chec..		-4,000.00	0.00
10/08/20	Payment	Bridget O Brien:New Grant	12000 Undeposited F	11000 Accounts Receivable		5,000.00	5,000.00
Total for Undeposited Funds						$5,000.00	
TOTAL						$5,000.00	

Looking through the detail, you can see the sales receipts go in and related deposit subtracted for all but one of the amounts. To correct this, go to +New, OTHER, Bank Deposit. This gives you a list of all of the undeposited amounts. If the deposit is there, make the deposit and go back to the **Statement of Financial Position**. It should now be refreshed with the undeposited amount as $0.

If you don't see the transaction on the **Bank Deposit** screen, go Reports, Reports, Deposit Detail.

Deposit Detail ✏️   [Switch to classic view]   [More actions ∨]   [Export / Print ∨]   [Save As]

All Dates ∨   Group ❶   ▽ Filter   ↕↕ General options   ⧉ Columns   ⊝

Deposit Detail ⋮
All Dates

Account ◇	Date ◇	Transaction type	Customer full name ◇	Ve... ◇	Descri... ◇	Clr	Amount ◇
Cash & Invest	09/27/..	Deposit	-	-	-	Uncleared	550.00
Total for Cash & Invest							$510.00
∨ Checking Account (12)							
Checking Account	10/03/...	Deposit		-	-	Uncleared	57,000.00
Checking Account	10/03/...	Deposit				Uncleared	-53,000.00
Checking Account	10/03/...	Deposit				Uncleared	-54,000.00
Checking Account	10/04/...	Deposit				Uncleared	$21.40
Checking Account	10/04/...	Deposit				Uncleared	-$21.40
Total for Checking Account							$20,000.00

Check date of deposits and adjust as needed.

This reports will list all of the Cash and Investment accounts that have had deposited posted for the dates requested. Check the date of your and see if the deposit was made by the end of the month. If the deposit was recorded as being put in the bank on the first day of the next month, the $5,000 should stay in Undeposited Funds. If it was deposited earlier, double click on the transaction and change the transaction date to the date of the actual deposit.

Next, print out the **Accounts Receivable Aging Report** from the Reports Center. The date of the report should be the closing date. This report should tie to the receivable amounts. Review any outstanding balances that are overdue.

Continuing down the **Statement of Financial** Position, you may see prepaid expenses. If so, drill down on the balance to see what is included. It may be used to record property or liability insurance or items needed for a fundraising event that won't occur until next year.

A journal entry is required to move the expense out of the prepaid asset account and into an expense account (+*New, OTHER, Journal Entry*). Here is an example entry.

Journal date			Journal no.			Is Adjusting Journal Entry?	
11/30/2020			1102				

#	ACCOUNT	DEBITS	CREDITS	DESCRIPTION	NAME	CLASS	
1	7240 Salaries & related expens	1,250.00		Nov prepaid expenses	Unrestricted	921 Salaries Cost Pool	🗑
2	7250 Salaries & related expens	100.00				921 Salaries Cost Pool	🗑
3	8260 Occupancy expenses:Equ	500.00				911 Facilities Cost Pool	🗑
4	8520 Misc expenses:Insurance	100.00				521 Governance	🗑
5	8520 Misc expenses:Insurance	200.00				911 Facilities Cost Pool	🗑
6	1450 Prepaid expenses		2,150.00				🗑
	Total	2,150.00	2,150.00				

In the example above, the organization is paying various expenses in advance—copier rental, insurance, health benefits, etc.—and then charging them to the programs monthly. If the amount is the same each month, it should be memorized and automated.

To make certain the ending balance in the prepaid accounts is correct, you would need to go through the details and see what amount is leftover in each area. Set up a spreadsheet to summarize the balance by type and print it out.

	A	B	C	D
1		We Care Community		
2		Prepaid Balance		
3		11/30/.		
4				
7		Property Insurance	1000	
8		D&O Insurance	4750	
9		HMO for Dec.	1250	
10		Total Acct 1450 Prepaid	$ 7,000	
11				

If you update it each month, this simple spreadsheet will save you lots of time at year end when the auditors want to know what is in the account. It will also keep you from overcharging the expense accounts.

I recommend setting up subaccounts for insurance, postage, and any other recurring prepaid expenses. You will still need to review them on a monthly basis, but it should go much quicker.

Print out the **Accounts Payable Aging** report from the **Vendors** reports for the accounts payable balance. The credit card balance will be any charges entered not yet paid. Continue down the balance sheet this same way, documenting the balances.

You will really impress your treasurer (or your auditor) if you hand him a package each month of the balance sheet with supporting documentation for each line of the balance sheet.

C. ALLOCATE FUND BALANCES

The bottom of the balance sheet has only one equity line called **Net Income**. But you need to know how much is in your restricted versus non-restricted net assets. To do this, run a **Profit & Loss (Statement of Activity) by Class** report for the same time period. Be sure to select the **CASH** basis of accounting.

Your Nonprofit
Statement of Activity by Class
December 2023

	100 ADMINISTRATION	100 CHILDREN'S PROGRAMS	900 FUNDS	910 WITHOUT RESTRICTIONS	920 WITH DONOR RESTRICTION	TOTAL
▾ Revenue						
43400 Direct Public Suppc		13,000.00		240.00	260,000.00	$277,240.00
Total		9.00				$00.00
Total Revenue	$0.00	$13,020.00	$0.00	$290.00	$260,000.00	$277,310.00
▾ Expenditures						
60900 Business Expe		2,700.00				$2,500.00
99200 Reserve Additions				1,000.00		$1,000.00
Total Expenditures	$445.00	$2,744.05	$0.00	$1,133.00	$500.00	$4,822.05
NET OPERATING REVENUE	$-445.00	$10,275.95	$0.00	$-843.00	$259,500.0	$272,487.95
NET OTHER REVENUE	$0.00	$0.00	$0.00	$1,000.00	$0.00	$1,000.00
NET REVENUE	$-445.00	$10,275.95	$0.00	$157.00	$259,500.00	$273,487.95

The Total figure will tie to **a Balance Sheet/Statement of Financial Position** for the same period. Monthly, you can review this report to see the breakout between funds **With and Without donor restrictions**, but at least annually, a journal entry will be necessary to reclassify the funds into their net asset accounts. I recommend having an outside accountant prepare these entries as there are accounting procedures relating to the release of net assets from restrictions. I won't bother you with an accounting lesson here, but if you decide to prepare the journal entry yourself, here is a basic example.

QBO records all the net income into the general (unrestricted) equity account. My example reclasses the restricted balance of $259,500 from the without restriction equity account to the restricted account. This reduces the balance in the without restriction net asset and increases it in the restricted net asset account.

D. RESTRICTED VERSUS UNRESTRICTED CASH

Another important item to review is the restricted versus unrestricted cash. If you have used the subaccount method, you will see your restricted cash on the detail balance sheet. Otherwise, you'll need to design a report showing the cash basis of the various funds. For those of you who have used this report in the desktop version, please note that QBO handles reports differently, so it will take a few more steps.

Go to *Reports, Business Budget vs Actuals* and select *Customize*. You will see a screen similar to this one.

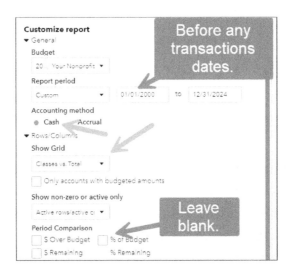

Let's fill out this screen from the top. The budget will default to your last budget. Leave it be as we won't be using the budget data. The **Report period** needs to include ALL the data. Fill in the first field with a date earlier than any transactions you've ever posted. The second date field needs the month-end or year-end date you are looking for. If the system requires a date in the first box, use the earliest date you have transactions in the system.

The **Accounting method** must be *Cash.* **Number format** can be your preference. Under **Rows/Columns, Show Grid,** select *Classes vs. Total.* Leave **Only accounts with budgeted amounts** unchecked as well as all the **Period Comparison** options.

Scroll down a bit further to the **Filter** option. Check the **Account** box and scroll down the list of accounts from the drop-down arrow until you see the individual accounts. Select **all** the accounts **except** cash, investment, receivables, and payables (including payroll). Include the buildings, equity, and all the revenue and expense accounts. I'll warn you, this is a bit tedious, so be sure to save the customizations when you are through.

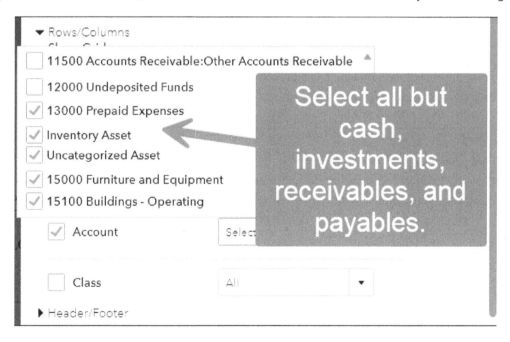

After you have selected all the accounts, look for the **Class** option. Leave it unchecked. Next change the report title under the **Header/Footer** option and *Run report. Save customization* so you don't have to do that again! Now let's look at the report.

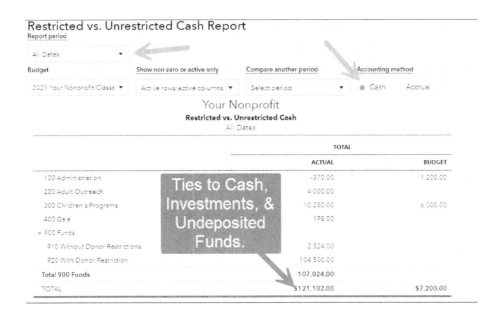

If you have a **Not Specified** line, these are transactions without associated classes. Click on the amount and go through the transaction report. Assign classes to the transactions as needed and rerun the **Restricted vs. Unrestricted Cash** report. The **TOTAL** on this report should match the total cash, undeposited funds, and investments on your balance sheet. If it does not, you have probably not selected all the accounts under **Filter** properly. Go back to the Customization area and carefully look through your filters.

The report includes budget columns you don't need, and you may want to group the funds differently. Now, you can "clean up" the report by exporting it into Excel, using the **share** icon discussed in Chapter 13. Once in the spreadsheet, delete the extra columns and group the classes together to show subtotals of unrestricted and restricted.

E. YEAR-END ADJUSTING ENTRIES

Any year-end journal entries outside of the normal monthly entries, including the audit adjusting entries, should be recorded as of the last day of the accounting period (12/31/xx, if using a calendar year). If possible, record all regular donations and checks prior to that day (12/30/xx), so you know anything recorded on the last day of the year is an adjustment. This will allow you to run reports with and without the adjustments by changing the date.

F. BOARD REPORTS

Speaking of the governing board, I recommend you put together the following monthly reports for them and offer any more details as needed:

- Balance Sheet or Statement of Financial Position
- Budget versus Actual
- Profit & Loss (Statement of Activities) by Class
- Funds Summary showing Restricted vs Non-Restricted Cash.

> *Additionally, you may wish to do some analysis and ratios showing:*
> - *percentage of dues received to date*
> - *percentage of donations received to budgeted amount.*

G. YEAR-END CLOSING

After you have completed your year-end tasks, you will want to lock the data so no one can change it. This is what accountants call closing the books. In QBO, there is not a true locking of the numbers. Instead, the data is password protected and warnings are issued if you try to post something to a closed period.

A closing date needs to be designated. From the *Gear* icon, select *YOUR COMPANY, Account and Settings, Advanced, Accounting.*

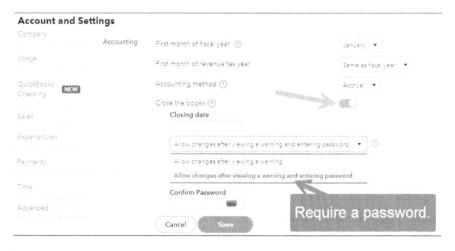

Select *Close the books* and choose a **Closing date,** entering the date of the last fiscal year or month. From the drop-down menu below it, choose to *Allow changes after viewing a*

warning and entering password. This option allows you to make prior period changes but requires a password. Choose a password that makes you think to yourself, "Do *I really want to do this?*", like *CallAccountant*.

> *If you forget the closing date password, the system will let the administrator delete it in the screen above and enter a new one. So protect the administrator's password!*

H. YEAR-END DONOR ACKNOWLEDGMENTS

Another year-end task is acknowledging the donations made by your donors and members. IRS regulations require organizations to provide acknowledgement for any donation over $250 and thanking your donors regularly for their support is always a good idea.

Additionally, you can use this communication as an internal accounting control tool and pledge reminder. As a control tool, consider sending donors who pledge or tithe a list of contributions and remaining balance quarterly. On the form should be a message to contact a designated person not involved in the bookkeeping if there is a problem with their statement. Increasing communication to thank your donors throughout the year is also a good idea.

For any discrepancies brought to your organization's attention, the designated person should meet with the bookkeeper and investigate. If the donor has made a donation that has not been recorded, the designated person will need to see if the check ever cleared the donor's bank and, if so, who endorsed it.

> *The donation may have been lost in the mail, accidentally posted to the wrong donor, or the bookkeeper may have stolen the money. Regardless, this would have been hard to catch without sending out the acknowledgment letters.*

Donor acknowledgment reports are designed from the **Sales by Donor Detail** (or **Sales by Customer Detail**) report. This report will show all money received by specific donors for the designated period, whether they were entered through sales receipts or payments on invoices.

Find this report by selecting *Reports* and scroll down to *Sales and customers* or search the Reports area. Open the report and click the pencil icon to change the report name to **Annual Donations** (or whatever you'd like).

Because not all monies your organization has received are tax deductible (like dues, book purchases, tuition for example), we need to filter the report to leave those items out of the report. Go to *Filter, Product/Service*.

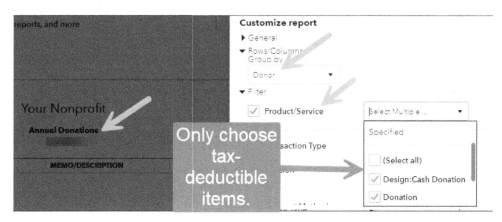

This will bring up a screen to choose the Products/Services you set up in Chapter 7. For this to work correctly, select only those items that the IRS considers deductible contributions. Click *Run report* when done.

On the report screen, choose the *Report period*. *Group by* should be Donor as this will set subtotals for each donor. Select *Cash Basis* for the **Accounting Method**. The *Gear* icon will let you change the columns displayed and reorder them.

As you are sending this to your donor, you only need the **Date, Transaction Type, Product/Service,** and **Amount**. Click *OK* when done to go back to the main customize screen.

To review your report, select *Run Report*.

Your Nonprofit
Annual Donations

DATE	TRANSACTION TYPE	PRODUCT/SERVICE	AMOUNT	BALANCE
▾ Aaron E Berhanu				
09/25/2019	Receipt	Design:Design	200.00	200.00
09/26/2019	Pledge	Sales	1,234.00	1,434.00
09/30/2019	Receipt	Donation	4,000.00	5,434.00
Total for Aaron E Berhanu			$5,434.00	
▾ Bridget O Brien				
▾ New Grant				
10/08/2019	Pledge	Donation	5,000.00	5,000.00
Total for New Grant			$5,000.00	
Total for Bridget O'Brien			$5,000.00	
▾ Byran Tublin				

This report shows each donor and their donations in one report. You need to separate this information in order to mail it out to donors. To do this, we will export the report to an Excel spreadsheet and insert page breaks. But before doing so, remember to **Save Customizations**.

Now select *Export* to send the report to Excel to see a spreadsheet like this one.

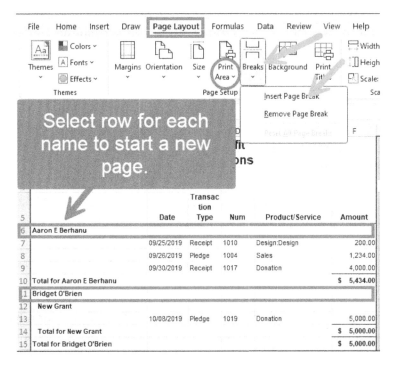

Under the *Page Layout* tab, select the entire row with the donor name. Select *Breaks, Insert Page Break,* and a break will be inserted just above that line. Repeat this for every donor.

Highlight the rows from the first donor to the last total for the last donor and over to the last column used. From the Excel top menu, select the drop-down arrow at *Print Area* and *Set Print Area.* Do not include the total line in the print area.

Back to the **Page Setup** box, go to **Print titles.** A pop-up box will show you the cells for the print area you had selected. If they are not correct, fix them here. The next line is **Print titles**. and click on the box next to *Rows to repeat at the top.* Select the header rows from the spreadsheet you want to print on the acknowledgment form.

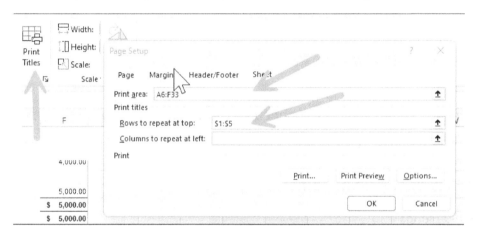

On the **Footer** tab of the **Page Setup** box, enter a thank you message.

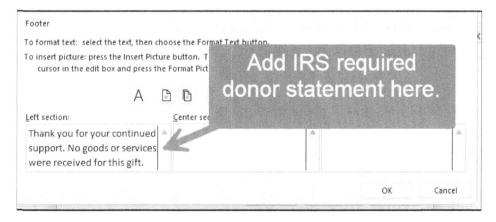

It is also a good idea to include the IRS required statement, i.e. *The donor did not receive goods or services in exchange for their donation.* (Unless they did, which has other acknowledgement rules. For details on acknowledging donor contributions, check out the IRS website or *Church Accounting—the How-To Guide for Small & Growing Churches.* Click *OK* when done.

Finally go to the top of the spreadsheet and select File, Print, Print Preview to view the pages of your reports.

We Care Community Foundation
Sales by Donor Detail
January - December 2020

	Date	Transaction Type	Product/Service	Amount
Jimenez, Cristina				
	01/10/2020	Sales Receipt	Individual contribution	100.00
	02/15/2020	Sales Receipt	Individual contribution	200.00
	06/20/2020	Sales Receipt	Individual contribution	40.00
Total for Jimenez, Cristina				$ 340.00

Thank you for your continued support

Each donor acknowledgment will print on its own page. When you are ready, print and mail reports with a cover letter.

I.   OTHER YEAR-END REQUIREMENTS

1. 1099 Filings

Organizations of all types pay people for services. If these people are not employees or work for a corporation, they are considered an independent contractor. There is a link to the IRS documents regarding rules for independent contractors at www.accountantbesideyou.com/irs-forms. *Church Accounting—The How-To Guide* also details this.

Annually, the IRS requires all organizations to send a Form 1099 to independent contractors paid over $600 (as of the time of this writing). Additionally, Form 1096 must be sent to the IRS with copies of the 1099s. Please refer to the IRS website or ask your accountant for the most current filing requirements.

The good news is QBO makes it easy to send these forms but only in the Plus and Advanced versions. When you set up your vendors in chapter 6, the Vendor Information screen had a box labeled **Track payments for 1099**.

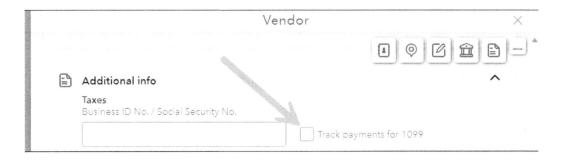

Before generating the 1099s, you will want to go back through your vendors and, for any that meet the IRS requirements, make sure you have selected that box.

To create 1099s, go to the left **Menu** bar and select *Expenses*, *Vendors*. You may have already noticed the *Prepare 1099s* button next to the **New vendor** button as shown below.

Select *Prepare 1099s* to bring up QBO's 1099 Wizard. Select *Let's get started* for the first step.

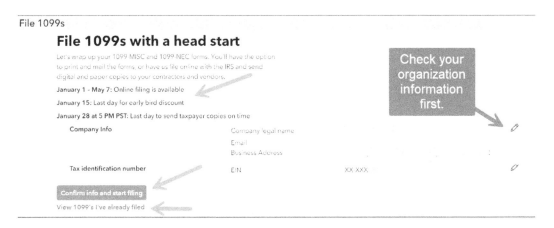

Verify that your organization's Employee ID (EIN), organization name, and legal address are all correct. You can make corrections if necessary by clicking on the edit pencil to the right of *Name and address* or *Tax ID*. This information **must be correct** because it will be used on the actual IRS 1099 and 1096 forms. There is also information about filing dates. You can **View 1099's I've already filed** to see if they have already been done. Select *Confirm info and start filing* when done.

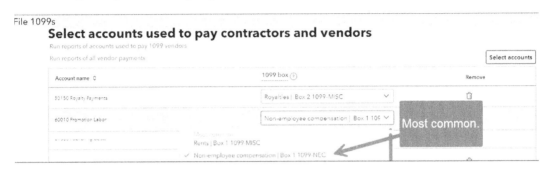

Next, a list of accounts that apply to your vendor payments will appear with a checkbox representing a box on the 1099-MISC and NEC forms. These categories are defined by the IRS. The most common 1099 category for small organizations is **Box 1: Nonemployee Compensation**. If you're not sure which category to choose, talk to your accounting professional or review the Form 1099 instructions found at IRS.gov.

 For more detailed information on completing the 1099s, check out my books, Nonprofit Accounting for Volunteers, Treasurers, and Bookkeepers and Church Accounting-The How-to-Guide for Small & Growing Churches.

Click *Next* to see the selected vendors, tax ID numbers, and addresses.

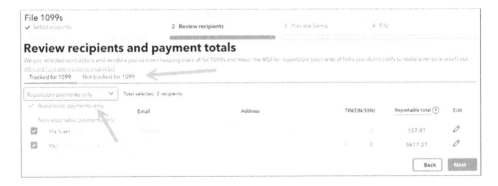

Review the vendor and details listed to assure they are accurate. Click *Edit* to the right of each Vendor if corrections are needed. Beware that making changes to your list from this screen will clear the **Track payments for 1099** check box in the vendor profile.

Notice the tab **Not tracked for 1099**. This will list all vendors paid but the **Track payments for 1099** box was not checked. If you see one that should be included, select *Add to tracked list*.

Even if you don't have the tax ID numbers of some vendors, go through the Wizard. It will show you which vendors were paid enough to need a 1099 and how many 1099 forms you will need to order. Select **Save and finish later** *and contact the vendors for any missing information. You can return to the Wizard when you have the data.*

Click *Next* to view vendors whose payments meet the threshold.

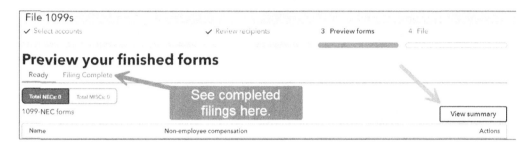

If the vendors from the previous screen did not show up here, it was because they were below the annual threshold. For any vendor and amount listed, you can click on it to open the 1099 Transaction Detail by Vendor report to see the payments that made up the total amount. You can drill down on any entry to see the transactions included for any vendor slated to receive a 1099.

The **Filing Complete** tabs lets you see any 1099s you have already filed. The **View summary** button give you a sheet of the data to be filed for review. This will list the vendors and show which are missing information. The **Tax ID** and the **Address** columns need to be complete and correct as they will be printed on the forms and mailed to the vendor and the IRS.

Select *Next* to file or print forms. A screen will appear asking if you want to E-file or print. Intuit will walk you through the necessary steps if you choose to E-file. To print, you will need to purchase a set of QBO compatible 1099 and 1096 blank forms to print them. These are often pricey; so if you only have a few to fill out, you may wish to order free forms from the IRS and fill them out by hand. The IRS free forms will not work with the 1099 wizard in QBO. QBO versions of the forms can be purchased at office supply stores or from online vendors including Intuit.

2. File W-2s for Employees

From the IRS website www.irs.gov/uac/Form-W-2,-Wage-and-Tax-Statement:

Every employer engaged in a trade or business who pays remuneration, including noncash payments of $600 or more for the year (all amounts if any income, social security, or Medicare tax was withheld) for services performed by an employee must file a Form W-2 for each employee (even if the employee is related to the employer) from whom: Income, social security, or Medicare tax was withheld. Income tax would have been withheld if the employee had claimed no more than one withholding allowance or had not claimed exemption from withholding on Form W-4, Employee's Withholding Allowance Certificate.

If you are using QuickBooks payroll or an outside payroll service, they should prepare and mail the W-2s to employees and file Form W-3, the summary transmittal, to the IRS with copies of the W-2s.

If you are not using an outside service, you will need to do this manually. For purposes of this book, I'm going to assume you are using an outside service.

Summary

Month ends and year ends are busy times for the accountants of an organization. In this chapter you were given a month and year-end checklist and learned how to:

- review your transactions,
- allocate fund balances,
- compute restricted versus unrestricted cash,
- make year-end adjusting entries,
- prepare board reports,
- set up a year-end closing control,
- prepare year-end donor acknowledgments,
- and prepare 1099s.

Great job! You've made it through all of the transactions for a year and know how to design and produce reports. In the next chapter, I'll go over some miscellaneous tasks that may come up.

15

SPECIAL TOPICS

You now understand the basics of setting up your accounting system and how to run it efficiently. In this chapter, you'll learn how to account for a few unusual items, about useful system features, and how to design reports for your annual audit. You can also check Accountantbesideyou.com for updated information and downloads to assist you.

A. HOW DO I ACCOUNT FOR ...???

1. Fundraisers

The most basic way to account for fundraisers is to have a class for each one that tracks the income and related expenses for the fundraiser. That works well if your fundraisers are a substantial portion of your organization's income and expenses (i.e. a foundation who raises money for a school through fundraisers) and you only have one or two a year. If it isn't a significant portion of your donations, then I recommend a process for tracking fundraisers that may seem a bit odd.

When you have a fundraiser, the board doesn't typically ask for the details of ticket sales versus sponsorship, etc. They want to know how much money the fundraiser netted (money in, less the money paid out). To do this, set up a parent account with an income type for each fundraiser. There can be as few as two subaccounts or as many as your system will hold. Below, I have set up a parent account for **Fundraising Income**.

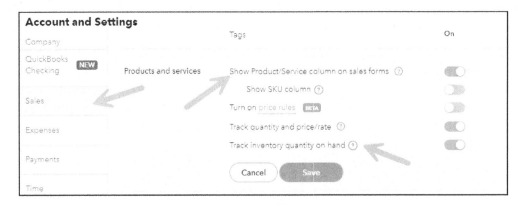

Under it are two events, and each event has a revenue and an expense title in the subaccount. The unusual thing is that I gave the expenses lines an income type. This is called a **contra-income** account and will show as a negative number. By subtracting the expense from the income, only the net profit from each fundraiser shows up on the financial statements.

If you would like to track the types of revenues received or detail types of expenses from a fundraiser, set up **Product/Services (Items)** for each (sponsorship, ticket sales, printing, advertising, etc.) and point them to these accounts. Reports can then be run on the items separately.

2. **Record the Sale of Merchandise**

Some organizations sell merchandise related to their programs. Depending on your program and your state, there may be tax consequences. Please see a local accountant to be certain you are following all the rules.

If you maintain inventory, there are some specific ways to record the purchase of the goods and the related sales. First you need to set the company preferences to allow for inventory. From the *Gear Icon*, select *YOUR COMPANY, Account and settings, Sales*. Click on the pencil icon in the **Product and services** section.

Click on the boxes next to *Show Product/Service* column on sales forms, *Track quantity and price/rate, Track inventory quantity on hand* and *Save*. **Turn on price rules** is a new feature that allows you to set discounts for specific customers.

Now that you have turned these settings on, go to the *Gear Icon, LISTS, Products and services*. Select *New* at the top right corner to create a new product. For this example, you will choose the **Inventory** option.

Enter the **Name** of the item you are selling. **SKUs** and **Categories** were discussed in Chapter 7. Use them as you see fit. Add a **Class** especially if the sales are for a particular program. Enter 0 for the **Initial quantity on hand.** If you already have stock, enter it as an inventory purchase in the previous year so as not to mess up your balance sheet.

Choose an **Inventory asset account and** enter the description you would like to see on invoices in the **Sales information** box. The **Sales price/rate** should be the regular sales price, keeping in mind it can be overridden. Choose the **Income account.** Input the **Cost** and link the **Expense account** to your Cost of goods sold (COGS). *Save and close.*

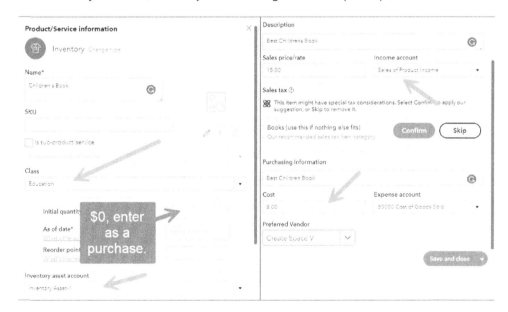

When you receive the bill for the inventory, go to *+New, VENDORS, Bill* and type in the vendor name.

Collapse the **Category details** section and go to the **Item details.** Under **Product/Service**, choose the inventory item and fill in the quantity **(QTY)**. The system will fill in the cost. If the CLASS does not auto populate, remember to include it. Click *Save* and the inventory will be recorded.

When a book is sold, enter the sale through *+New, Customers, Sales Receipt*. Enter the sale just like you did with Donations, but use the **Product/Service** of *Childrens Book* instead. Double check that the **Class is filled in.** If sales tax is required, QBO will step you through the process. You can toggle the sales tax on and off for non-taxable sales. Be sure to work with a local accountant to ensure you are charging and remitting the correct amount of state and local taxes.

Once the purchases and sales have been saved, QBO will record the inventory and the cost of goods sold (COGS), leaving a net profit on books.

My Nonprofit
Sales by Product/Service Summary
January 1-30, 2024

	QUANTITY	AMOUNT	% OF SALES	AVG PRICE	COGS	GROSS MARGIN	GROSS MARGIN %
			TOTAL				
Annual Dues	2.00	100.00	0.13 %	50.00			
Children's Book	5.00	75.00	0.10 %	15.00	40.00	35.00	46.67 %
in Dues							
Returned Check	1.00	50.00	0.07 %	50.00			
TOTAL		$75,550.00	100.00 %		$40.00		

To find this reports, go to *Reports, Sales and customers,* **Sales by Product/Service Summary.** **Product/Service List** is also useful to see your quantity on hand. Also note the quantity will be automatically reduced by the sale of any books.

3. In-Kind Donations

There are times organizations receive donations of items or professional services instead of cash. These are called in-kind donations. Typical examples of in-kind donations are computers, paintings, office supplies, legal services (this is only considered an in-kind donation if the organization would have otherwise had to pay for the service) or use of space without being charged rent.

 *Every organization should have written guidelines for accepting **in-kind donations**. You do not have to accept everything that is offered. If it cannot be used or sold, do not accept it.*

When you receive an in-kind gift, it is appropriate to acknowledge it. However, do not value the gift in the acknowledgement; simply thank them for the item. For the donor's tax purposes, valuation is the donor's responsibility. An exception to that rule is the donation of a car, boat, or plane received for resell. For details on how to handle this, read *Church Accounting–The How-to Guide* or *Nonprofit Accounting for Volunteers, Treasurer & Bookkeepers* or call your accountant and ask how to handle tax implications and reporting of vehicle donations.

To record an in-kind donation in QBO, set up an income account titled *In-Kind Contribution* and an expense account titled *Donated Goods & Services*. If you plan to use the items donated, you can enter the transaction as a journal entry or as a sales receipt.

If you enter it as a sales receipt, you will need to set up items related to the donation. This method is useful if you have a large number of in-kind donations and would like to run an item report to see what types of goods are being received. Otherwise, it is probably easier to record it as a journal entry.

Go to *+New, OTHER, Journal Entry.*

#	ACCOUNT	DEBITS	CREDITS	DESCRIPTION	NAME	CLASS	
1	6800 Donated Goods and Services	100.00		Donated Computer		Admin	
2	4380 In Kind Contribution		100.00	Donated Computer		Without Donor Restrictions	

Use your best estimate to value the donation. Charge the donated goods expense line as a **DEBIT** and the in-kind contribution as a **CREDIT** for the same amount, assigning it to the appropriate program or fund. *Save and close* when you are finished.

If you are using the donated goods or services, you don't need to do anything else in QBO. However, if you sell the donated item, you will need to record the sale. Go back to the journal entry screen.

This time, **DEBIT** the checking account where the money received was deposited and **CREDIT** the donated goods expense. You must be certain to assign the donated goods to the same program under **Class** as the original entry.

4. Record a Mortgage

If your church has a mortgage, you will need to set up a few accounts before you get started. Go to *Gear, YOUR COMPANY, Chart of Accounts* to add the following (if you haven't already):

- a Fixed Asset account to record the building or land. This may also be called Construction in Progress for a building under construction
- a Long-Term Liability account to record the loan
- a Prepaid Asset account for any escrow payments
- Expense accounts for any loan expenses.

Additionally, you will need to set up your mortgage company as a vendor. Set up a new **Service** item (*Gear, LISTS, Products and Services, New*) called **Mortgage.**

Select *I sell this product*... and use the drop-down arrow under **Income account** to select the *Mortgage* liability account you previously set up.

When you receive the money for the loan, enter it through **Sales Receipt** (+New, CUSTOMERS, Sales Receipt), with the mortgage holder as your vendor and use the Product/Service you just set up.

To make loan payments, go to +New, Vendors, Bill. Select the mortgage holder as the **Vendor.**

Using either the notice from the bank or an amortization schedule, split the payment between principal and interest payments. If you have an escrow, record it to the escrow account. Use *Make recurring* to remind you to book the entry each month. You will need to adjust the principal and interest numbers each time, but it will save you entering the rest of the data.

5. A Reserve Account on the Income Statement

Many organizations like to set up a reserve at a bank and designate an amount of money to be transferred to that account on a monthly or quarterly basis. Because the reserve account is a bank or investment account, the transfer of the funds does not show on the income statement.

If your governing board or treasurer would like to see the amount of money moved to the reserve account on the income statement of the general fund, add two accounts to your chart of accounts list: **Reserve Transfer Deposit** and **Reserve Additions**. Add the accounts by going to the *Gear, YOUR COMPANY, Chart of Accounts, New*. Select **Income** icon at the top for the **Category Type**, then select the *Other Income* from the drop-down menu. The **Tax form section** can be *Other Miscellaneous Income*.

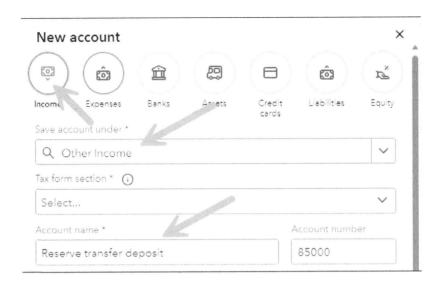

The deposit account must have an account type of *Other Income* in order to show below the operating expense line. Save this account and enter the payment account.

Next set up an **Expenses** account called **Reserves Additions**.

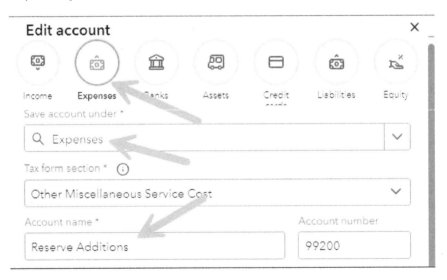

This time you will select a **Category** type of *Expenses* with a **Save account under** of *Expenses* and the **Tax form section** can be *Other Miscellaneous Expense*. Save the entry.

When you write the check to make the transfer, instead of assigning it to the investment account, charge it to the **Reserve Additions** account. To record the check, go to *Plus, Vendors, Check* and use the general fund or unrestricted class. The Payee will be **Transfer** as discussed in Chapter 11. Make the deposit by going to *+New, Other, Bank Deposit*.

On the screen to input deposits, you will change the **Deposit to** account in the upper left corner to your investment account where the money was transferred. Under **Add funds to this deposit**, the **ACCOUNT** should be the *Reserve transfer deposit* account.

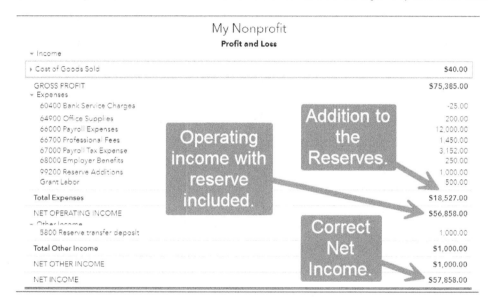

Once saved, your overall income statement will show the expense in operations and the deposit as other income.

6. Interfund transfers

When an organization receives a donation, it is recorded in the fund or program it was designated for or into the general fund. If the governing board decides to allocate some of the unrestricted funds into a specific program, you will need to record an interfund transfer.

Set up a new **Other Expense** account called Inter-fund Transfers. Then go to *Gear, OTHER, Journal entry*. Record a debit to the Inter-fund account for the amount being transferred with the **CLASS** of the fund **giving** the money (General or Admin). On the next line, use the same Inter-fund account, but change the **CLASS** to the **receiving** fund. This will have a net impact of $0 on the cash and the overall financial picture, but will show more funds available in the receiving fund.

7. **Stock Donations**

NOTE: This and the next section were originally recorded as a post at my QuickTips Blog at AccountantBesideYou.com.

Does your nonprofit encourage donations of stock? If not, you should. **Transferring stock for a charitable contribution** may give the donor a significant tax advantage. With the stock market at all-time highs, many donors may have stock that has grown in value over the last few years. By donating the actual stock instead of selling it, the donor will not have to pay capital gains on the appreciation. This is a win for both the donor and the organization.

Stock transferred as a donation to an eligible organization may be deducted by the donor at the market value as of the date of transfer, IF it has been held for over one year (If it was purchased less than one year ago, the contribution is limited to the purchase price of the stock). In order to understand how this helps your donors, let's walk through an example.

Assume I purchased 100 shares of a corporation five years ago for $15 per share. In 2024, the value is up to $30 per share. Assume I would like to give my church a $3000 donation. If I sell the stock, I will receive $3000 ($30 x 100 shares), but I owe the government capital gains tax on the $1500 increase in the value of the stock ($15 per share x 100 shares sold). So now, instead of having $3000 available to donate, if I'm in a 20% tax bracket, I only have $2250 available.

If I transfer the 100 shares directly to the church, I can still take the full $3000 charitable gifts deduction from my taxes, but I don't have to pay any capital gains tax, nor does the organization. For additional information, go to the IRS website http://www.irs.gov/publications/p526/ar02.html#en_US_2013_publink1000229755 or talk to a tax specialist.

Many times I've heard organizations say they don't accept stock transfers because they don't have an investment account. As a strong believer in making it easy for your donors to give you money for your mission, I encourage your organization to set one up immediately. Work with a local broker and you can quickly develop an easy set of instructions on how to transfer stock to your account.

Now here is the important part. Let your donors know about the option! Remind them to speak to their tax professional to get the best benefit. There should be a designated person in your organization as the point person for the donors if they have questions. And do NOT list your account number in an email or on your website. Let's not make life easy for hackers.

To record the receipt of stock in your accounting system, you will want to set up an invoice under the donor's name for the full market value of the stock. If the stock was used to pay a pledge that has already been entered, you can skip this step.

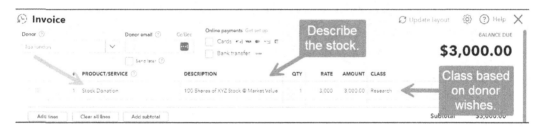

To record the receipt of the stock, go to *+New, CUSTOMER,* **Receive payment**. Enter the amount as the full market value. If there were brokerage expenses, we will record those later as the donor records need to reflect the full value before any transaction expenses. You may add a **Payment Method** called Stock.

The value of the stock on the brokerage report may be slightly less than the pledge. This often happens when there is a change in value from the time the donor authorized the transfer until it was recorded in your account. If it is a small amount, choose the write off option.

Next, you will need to go to **+New, OTHER, Bank Deposit**. Change the *Account* option to the investment account the stock was transferred into. After selecting the amount from the Payments screen, you can adjust the deposit for any transaction fees. Enter the fee amount as a negative number on the next line. You will also need to assign a general ledger account number to the adjustment under the FROM ACCOUNT. I usually prefer to use the same donation account where the invoice/pledge was recorded so the net donation will be correct.

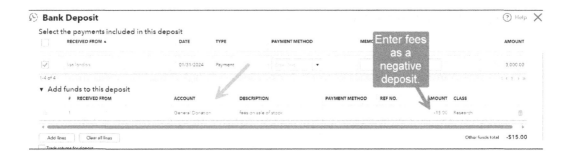

Save the deposit.

If your organization immediately sells the stock, make a journal entry to record the transfer by going to *+New, OTHER, Journal entry*. Debit the checking or other cash account for the amount received, credit the investment account for the amount of value you have it recorded at and debit any transaction or brokerage fees to **Bank Charges**. If the organization does a number of stock sales, set up an **Other Expense** account for **Investment Transaction Fees** to record the fees to instead.

Now the Statement of Financial Position (Balance Sheet) and Statement of Activities (Income Statement) reflect the donation properly.

If the stock was donated to fund an endowment, you may wish to keep this money in a separate account from other cash or investments. Between classes and accounts, assets and equity, it can get very confusing trying to figure out how to track all the related pieces of an endowment or memorial account. Let's separate the pieces to see how to record these in QuickBooks.

In this example, a generous donor has donated $10,000 of stock to seed an endowment fund. If you are going to keep this money in a separate bank account from your other investments, you will record the initial receipt as a Sales Receipt (or Payment on Invoice). Under the Make Deposit screen, select the appropriate Investment Account instead of the checking.

8. Investment Gains and Losses

Whether the donations of stock were given for endowments or general support, we need to record the investment earnings and change in values. If your nonprofit or church has investment accounts, you will notice on the brokerage statements the earnings may be divided into *Realized* and *Unrealized* Income. Realized income is money earned and received into your account. Typical examples are dividend income, interest income, gain (or loss) on the sale of stock. Unrealized income/loss reflects the impact of current market conditions on your holdings.

For example, assume the organization has 100 shares of stock in American Airlines it purchased at $40, for a book value of $4000. If the market price of American Airlines stock is $42 at the end of the quarter, the organization has an unrealized gain of $200 ($2 per share x 100 shares). If the stock price was $38, it would be an unrealized loss of $200. If American Airlines paid a 3% dividend, the $120 ($4000*.3%) would be a realized gain.

To keep your accounting records accurate, you will want the Statement of Financial Position and your Statement of Activities to reflect both the realized and the unrealized gains and losses. Many smaller organizations record them in a single investment income account, but I recommend showing the *realized* separate from the *unrealized* so the governing council can see what has actually been earned versus market fluctuations.

Using the example above, let's walk through a sample journal entry.

	Debit	Credi
1120-Investment Account	$320.00	
4520-Realized Gain/Loss Investment		$120.00
4530-Unrealized Gain/Loss Investment		$200.00

The class can be your general/administrative class, or, if the investment account is to support a specific program, the realized gain/loss should be coded to the appropriate program or fund class. I prefer to keep the unrealized gains and losses in the general/administrative class, so the program's financials aren't distorted by changing market conditions.

Often the earnings on an endowment can go to the general fund or other unrestricted use. Assuming $50 of quarterly earnings are to be transferred to the general fund, go to *Banking, Transfer Funds* to record the movement of the cash from the investment account to the general checking account.

After the transactions are recorded, the ending balance in the Investment Account should equal the ending balance on the brokerage statement.

9. Mission Trips or Member-Specific Accounts

If your organization offers mission trips or other events which the members raise money for their related expenses, there are a few extra steps to take. You will need to set up the system to track the fundraisers and revenue coming in by member and also track the expenses by member.

First let's add a **Product/Service** item called Mission Fundraiser. Go to *Gear, LISTS, Products and services, New, Service.* Point it to a Fundraising Income account. If you have a Fundraisers Class, add a new sub-class called Mission Trip. To do this, go to *Lists, Class List, Class, Add New.* When the new class box appears, select *Subclass of* and choose Fundraisers. If not, set up a Mission Trip class.

Next, add each person going on the trip as a Sub-donor called *Last name Mission Trip* or your preferred naming protocol. See Chapter 6 for how to setting up donors.

With these accounts set up, you are ready to record the money coming in. If the donation does not need to be kept under the donor's name (i.e. cash received at a fundraiser), use the sub-customer name of the person going on the mission trip in the sales receipt screen. Select the **Product/service** to be *Mission Fundraiser,* adjust the description as necessary, and use the new Mission Trip class or subclass.

If a fundraiser is being shared by several members, you can allocate the receipts among the different people going.

If a check or other donation was received, it needs to be under the actual donor's name. Check with your accountant to see if the donation is deductible or not. In this case, use the mission trip product/service item and the mission trip class under the actual donor's name. Then under the **attendee's** sub-donor name, create an invoice for the donation under the mission job and class and enter the amount of the donation. You now have the same donation in twice, so you'll need to enter a credit under the customer account of the attendee. Under *+New, Customers, Credit Memos,* issue a credit for the amount of the donation. This time use only the customer name, not the sub-donor. That way the sub-donor will show the donation, but the overall account for the person going does not show the additional amount. Be sure to use the same Mission Trip class.

When the trip expenses need to be paid, you will go to the **Bills** screen. In the following example, I'm assuming we bought tee shirts for the trip. The **Expense Account** is Other mission expenses. If this were the airline bill, it would be travel. Add additional sub-donors to split the costs. Notice the expense is allocated to everyone going on the trip via the **Donor/Project** column. The **Class** goes to the subclass for the mission trip. **Save & Close**.

To see how much money has been raised and spent by each member, we need to go to the **Profit and Loss by Donor** report. Customize the report by Class or Sub-class.

	AMY WHITE	MISSION TRIP	TOTAL AMY WHITE	LISA LONDON	MISSION TRIP	TOTAL LISA LONDON	TOTAL
My Nonprofit							
Profit and Loss by Donor							
January 2024							
▾ Income							
▾ 4200 Fundraising Income							$0
Total Income	$0	$1,000	$1,000	$0	$1,000	$1,000	$2,000
GROSS PROFIT	$0	$1,000	$1,000	$0	$1,000	$1,000	$2,000
▾ Expenses							
Other Mission Trip Expenses		20	20		20	20	$40
Total Expenses	$0	$20	$20	$0	$20	$20	$40
NET OPERATING INCOME	$0	$980	$980	$0	$980	$980	$1,960
NET INCOME	$0	$980	$980	$0	$980	$980	$1,960

From this report, we can see that Amy has raised $1000 towards the trip and has spent $20. Because they were set up as sub-donors, we also see a total for the donor. You may wish to export the report into Excel and delete the extra columns.

Once you know what each member has raised and spent, you may wish to know how the total trip is looking. To do this, you will design a *Profit & Loss Statement by Class* customized for the mission trip.

Go to *Reports* and search *Profit & Loss by Class*. When the report comes up, select *Customize* for the Mission trip or Fundraising class.

My Nonprofit
Profit and Loss by Class
January 2024

	FUNDRAISER	TOTAL
▾ Income		
▾ 4200 Fundraising Income		$0.00
Total 4200 Fundraising Income	2,000.00	$2,000.00
Total Income	$2,000.00	$2,000.00
GROSS PROFIT	$2,000.00	$2,000.00
▾ Expenses		
Other Mission Trip Expenses	40.00	$40.00
Total Expenses	$40.00	$40.00
NET OPERATING INCOME	$1,960.00	$1,960.00
NET INCOME	$1,960.00	$1,960.00

Save customization to save time next month.

10. Opportunity Scholarships

If your school receives scholarships from a governmental unit for specific children, you can track these in QuickBooks Online.

Assumptions:

Let's start by reviewing the assumptions. For this example, I assume:

1. the parents apply directly to the government or grantor for the scholarship
2. money is paid directly to the school
3. payments are received by semester from the grantor
4. if a student drops out, the scholarship money is prorated and given back to the grantor
5. the school bills in monthly installments and does not require the parents to pay if the student drops out.

Assumption #4 is important, because if the money must be returned if the student leaves, it is a liability (something owed) until it is earned.

Setup:

Start by setting up the governmental agency or grantor as a **Customer** or **Donor** with a **Donor type** of Government. Set up a **NEW Product/Service** as a Service type called *Scholarship* and point it to a liability account (2xxxx) called "Unearned/deferred tuition" or "Unearned Scholarships". If you could also track it by Tuition Scholarship, Books Scholarship, Fees Scholarship if you need specific reports for this, but they still all need to be pointed to a balance sheet liability account like "Unearned/Deferred Tuition".

Next decide if you will be tracking the individual students within QuickBooks or via a spreadsheet. If you have a large number of students receiving the scholarships, you may find tracking via spreadsheet is easier. If there are not many, keeping all the information in the same system is preferred.

If Tracking Student Scholarships by Spreadsheet:

For the **Spreadsheet approach**, invoice the Customer (i.e. the grantor) for the full amount of the scholarships expected for the semester using the Product/service item called *Scholarship* you just set up. When the payment is received, apply it against this invoice.

At that point, your balance sheet will show the cash in the bank and the related liability.

If Tracking Student Scholarships within QuickBooks:

If you want to track the scholarships with a **Within QuickBooks approach,** setup **sub-donors** under the Grantors Customer name using the student name. If you use numbers for the students, add them to the **Other** block in the **Name and contact** area.

Create an invoice for the scholarship awarded for each student, using the student sub-donor name and the Product/service item called *Scholarship* you just set up.

When the payment is received, apply each student's amount against the individual sub-donors.

Recording Tuition and Fees for Both Approaches:

When the school year starts, set up invoices by Parent:Student (not Grantor:Student) for the first month tuition, books, etc. Set up the 2nd month invoice for just tuition and any recurring charges and Memorize and Automate it to record monthly through the end of the school year. (You can always edit these later if something changes).

The invoices will record the tuition, fees, and books into your income and establish an Accounts Receivable. When you are paid by the parents, apply the payment to the invoice.

Allocate Scholarships to the Student Accounts Monthly:

Monthly, you will allocate the "earned" scholarship against the amount owed by the parents. To do this, go to **Customer, Create Credit Memos**. Enter the student as the Customer, **Product/service** will equal **Scholarship** (or whatever name you gave to the new item you set up earlier). This will take the money from Unearned tuition and apply it to the student's account. These credit memos can be memorized to be automated every month.

Student Drops Out and Money Must be Refunded to Grantor:

If a student drops out, you will need to Issue a refund check to the grantor. Go to *+New, CUSTOMER, Refund Receipt*, and put the Grantors name in the Customer area. If you are tracking within QuickBooks, this should be the Grantor:Student sub-donor.

The Product/service should be Scholarships, so the Unearned Tuition account is reduced by the amount of the repayment.

B. HOW DO I???

1. **Invite and Manage Multiple Users**

QBO allows you to set up and manage access for multiple users. Only a user designated as an administrator or who has been given user management permission can add a new user. QBO identifies each unique user by their email address, which also serves as their User ID.

The QBO Plus version supports up to 5 users, while QBO Advanced allows up to 25 users. **Reports Only** and **Time Tracking Only** users do not account against your user limits. Setting up users is an important process because it is where user access is controlled. Keeping in mind the importance of internal controls, I suggest you carefully consider what level access each user needs. To add a user, click the *Gear, Your Company, Manage users*.

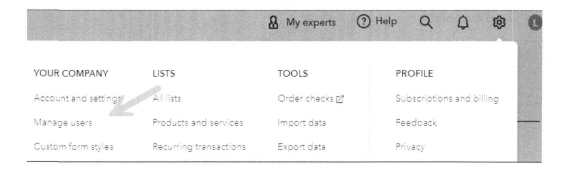

In the **Manage Users** screen, an administrator will see all users and their assigned user rights.

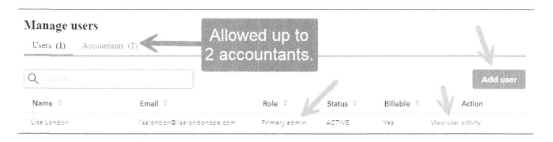

User can be added, edited, and deleted, or their system activity can be viewed from this screen. Invite up to two accountant users using the **Accounting firms** tab. Change the user access at any time under the **Action** column.

The **View User Activity** option allows you to review all of the users' QBO activity in the **Audit Log**. This log documents every activity performed under each user's login. Click the arrow in the **User** box to select an employee to review.

On your screen, you may notice some of the **Events** are listed in blue. These indicate that you can click on them to see the document that was changed.

Now let's add a new user and learn about access. Using the back arrow on your browser, go back to the **Manage users** screen and click the *Add user* button at the top.

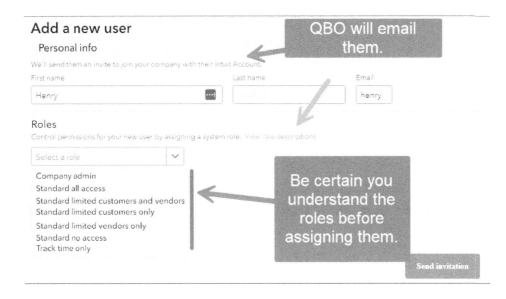

An interview screen opens to start the process of adding a new user. Here you will choose the user type to determine what level of access they need. Click on the *View role descriptions* for details of what each level entails.

A **Company administrator** has full access rights. **View company reports** users do not see or enter transactions but can view most reports. You may wish to set up your board of directors with **View company reports** rights. **Track time only** users can only view and enter their own time tracking information. Neither the reports nor time tracking only user count towards your licensed user number. Select *Next* to continue through the screens.

If you choose **Standard all access** user, you can scroll down to the **Add additional permissions** and decide if you want to allow the user to Access subscription or Manage users. Your average user will not normally need to manage users, edit company information or manage the subscriptions. Click *Send invitation* and enter the user's email address and name. The user will receive an email invitation and will be prompted to create a password.

If the user is already a QBO user, they will use their current password. By accepting the invite, they have access to your organization's file.

2. **Invite an Accountant**

You can invite your accountant to sign into your company file directly. This access allows your accountant to make changes at his or her convenience. The best part is you can both work in your data at the same time. Up to two accountants can be invited for free without counting toward your current user limit. These may include your bookkeeper, accountant, auditor, or tax professional.

The process for inviting your accountant is similar to the process above. Go to the **Manage Users** screen and select the **Accountants** tab. Click *Invite* in the upper right corner. You will enter your accountant's email address. QBO will email them and your accountant will be able to see and access your data.

3. Send a Thank You from the Receipts Screen

Thanking donors promptly is crucial for small nonprofits. You can email a donor a thank-you note directly from the sales receipt screen in QBO. It takes a bit of time to design and layout the template, but once you do, it is a huge timesaver.

Go to *Gear, Account and settings, Sales, Messages*. Click in the *Message* section or the *edit pencil* and the **Message** template screen will open.

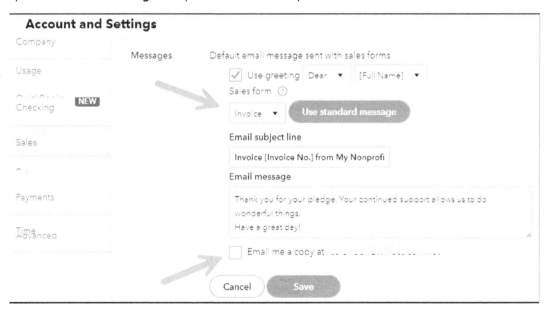

In this screen you can customize the email wording for messages that are sent with any Pledge/Invoice, Sales Receipt, or Statement. Select *Pledge* or *Sales Receipt* and make changes to the **Greeting**, **Subject,** and **Email message**.

You can enter a **Default** message (up to 1000 characters) that will appear on the sales receipt or other sales form. I recommend using this field to insert the standard IRS required wording for acknowledging donations. Click *Save* when done.

You will repeat the process of creating a message for each form by selecting that form name from the drop-down menu as shown above.

4. Customize Forms

You may also want to customize forms to match your organization's colors. You can change the layout of your forms and select what information you want the donor or member to see.

Customizations are found under *Gear, Your Company, Custom Form Styles.* This will bring you to the **Custom Form Styles** list.

This page will list any custom forms you have created. The only form now in the list is the default form. Click *New style, Sales receipt* to begin creating a new sales receipt.

You have lots of choices to customize your forms. Notice the top of the screen are three headings: **Design, Content,** and **Emails**. I'll walk you through each of these.

Let's begin with **Design**. Name your form template, and click on the icon that says **Dive in**. Click on each of the preset layout styles until you find the one you prefer. Next click on the **Make logo edits** icon to upload your logo, change its size and move its position.

Try other color allows you to pick the color scheme. Click on their offered colors or key in your brand's color numbers. As you change the colors, the sample invoice on the screen displays the new scheme.

The next icon allows you to change the fonts and sizes. **When in doubt, print it out** gives you the ability to change the margins, use letterhead, or fit the paystub in a window envelope. At the bottom of the screen, the **Preview PDF** button allows you to download and save or print the PDF.

The second tab is **Content**. This is where you will edit the body of the document. Start by selecting the small pencil icon in the corner of the section you want to change.

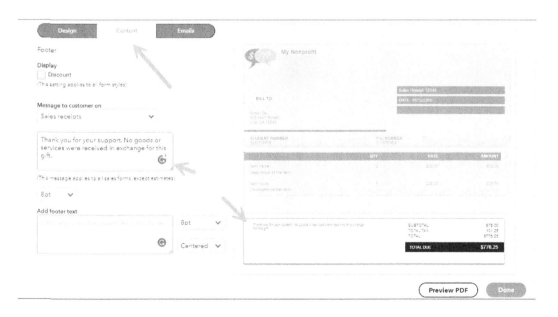

In the **Header** section, you will enter the report headings as you want them to appear on the various printouts and select how much information should be included. You can rename the forms and use form numbers here.

Explore the other options on this tab by selecting the pencil icons on the body and the footer. The **Table** section contains selections about the actual transaction. You will choose how much information about the donation or payment you want to see and how it will be displayed. Finally, the **Footer** section allows you to enter a message to all donors. Within the footer, I suggest you enter an appropriate IRS compliant statement

The next tab is **Emails**. At the top you can choose whether to have the body of the email show the transactions or just the balance due and whether or not to have the document attached as a PDF. I recommend attaching the PDF as it is more convenient for your donor to print out or save as a digital file that way.

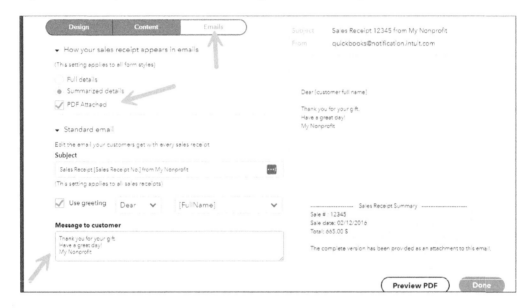

The **Standard email** can be customized as need as can the **Reminder email**. Select *Done* when you are finished.

5. Using the purchase order option on grants

Your donor may track their grants using a numbering system that you would like to have reflected on your correspondence. If so, you will want to add the PO field to your invoices.

If you are using Intuits standard invoice template, it already has the PO. If you are using the standard Pledge template, it does not. To modify the template, pull up an invoice (*+New, CUSTOMER, Invoice/Pledge*) and select the small *Gear* at the top. You may change the **PO No.** block to say **Grant No.** (or anything you like). Click on the pencil icon. Deselect any of the other categories you do not need. Save as a copy of the standard invoice and use with the appropriate donors.

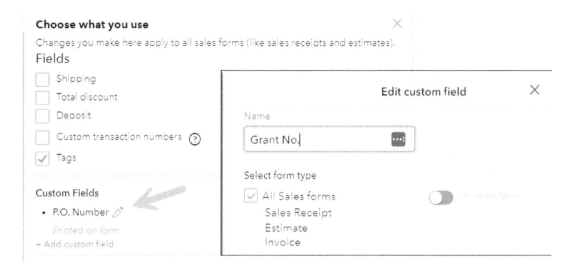

6. Merge duplicated donor or vendor accounts

While looking through the donor or vendor lists, you may find some duplicate donor or vendor names. This often occurs when the naming protocol isn't clear. Luckily, QuickBooks makes this easy to correct.

Go to *Sales, Donors*. Write down the exact customer name of the account you wish to keep, paying attention to spacing and capitalization for reference. Then double-click on the customer or job you don't want to use. This will bring up a window with an **Edit** box in the upper right. Click the arrow to get **Merge contacts**.

A pop-up box will appear with the name you clicked on as the customer to **Merge transactions** from. Use the drop-down arrow under the **Into** box and select the donor you want the data to go to. Click *Merge contacts*.

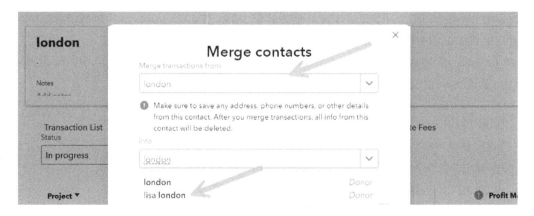

Please note that you cannot combine the names if they both have sub-donors. Delete or move the jobs from the customer name you will be removing before attempting the merge. Vendor names can be merged using the same process.

7. Give Feedback to QBO

I mentioned at the start of this book that QBO is automatically updated with the latest updates and improvements to the application. Most system improvements and enhancements originate from users like you. You may have noticed buttons that said **Share feedback** on various screens throughout the program. Please use them.

You can also go to *Gear, Profile, Feedback*. You may tell the QBO developers any ideas or bring bugs to their attention. Don't be afraid to enter your ideas. You never know what other churches or organizations may need the same thing. QBO also likes for users to vote on what enhancements they should work on adding next.

C. WHAT ABOUT ...???

1. Reports I Need for an Audit

Though every audit is different, there are some basic reports your auditor will probably request. Some are financial and others are managerial. In planning for your audit, I'd recommend you gather, print, or have in an electronic file the following information as of the last day of the period being audited:

- Board Minutes
- Contracts, including employment, rent, insurance, etc.
- Accounts receivable aging detail (list of amounts due from donors)
- Accounts payable aging detail (list of amounts due to vendors)
- Payroll reports from the outside service or detail files.

As I mentioned in Chapter 14, I'd recommend printing out the balance sheet and attaching the reconciliations for the bank and stock accounts and the credit cards. Make sure everything ties first!

Additionally, you will invite the auditor as your accountant as we learned in section 2 above of this chapter. This will give them full access to your company records to get the information they need. However, they may have questions and request documents to support your numbers in QBO.

2. Tax Stuff

I am not offering any tax advice. Even though nonprofits are considered tax exempt, they may have activities that are taxable or, at least, have reporting requirements. Download IRS Publication 598 (http://www.irs.gov/pub/irs-pdf/p598.pdf) for information on unrelated business income. Additionally, ask your local accountant or tax attorney if your organization has any taxable activities.

States may also have different taxing requirements, especially with sales tax. If you sell products (like books or clothing), you may be required to collect and remit these taxes. Furthermore, some states exempt organizations and nonprofits from paying sales taxes on their own purchases or they reimburse them for the taxes paid. As every state is different, I'm afraid it is outside the scope of this book to cover them all. Again, check with your local accountant.

Summary

This chapter was filled with lots of miscellaneous information I hope you found helpful. In it you learned how to:

- account for fundraisers,
- record the sale of merchandise,
- record in-kind donations,
- record a mortgage,
- set up a reserve account on the income statement,
- handle mission trips,
- record scholarships,
- invite and manage multiple users,
- invite an accountant,

- send a thank you from the receipts screen,
- customize forms,
- give feedback to QBO,
- and determine which reports you need for an audit.

We are almost finished. Now let's see how you can use your smartphone to access additional QBO features.

16

QBO APPS

Now that we have covered the basics of QBO, I will introduce you to some tools that expand its usefulness and accessibility. QBO can be accessed from your smartphone or mobile device. Also, QBO has third party apps that work with it to help further automate and organize your work.

D. QBO FROM YOUR MOBILE DEVICE

The QBO Mobile allows you to run your organization on the go! You are able to send invoices, capture receipts, or review transactions and balances from anywhere using your smartphone or tablet. The QBO app is available on both Android and Apple devices at no cost.

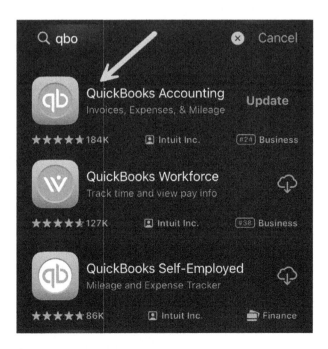

After the app is installed, the QBO icon will appear on your screen. Tap the icon to open it. Then sign in using the same User ID (email) and password that you use to log in on your PC.

The first time you log in, QBO wants to confirm that it's really you logging into a new device. QBO will send an email to your email address with a verification code to enter. After you check your email and enter that code, QBO opens to a screen with **Quick Actions** and **To do**.

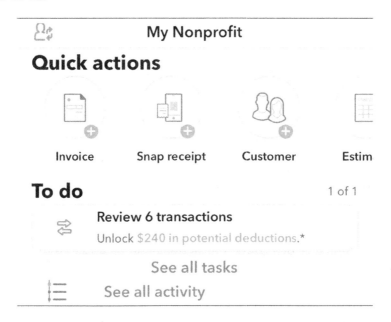

The **Quick Actions** allow you to start a new invoice, snap a receipt, add a customer, etc. **To do** shows you transactions that need to be reviewd. At the bottom right, click the three-line menu icon to open the **Shortcuts** and **All**. Using these menus, income and expense transactions, customers, vendors, products, and services are viewed or added. Note the QBO mobile app labels your **Donors** or **Members** as customers. You **CANNOT** edit or add accounts to your Chart of Accounts using your mobile device.

A very useful tool is the **Snap receipt**. Use it to take a picture of a receipt and QBO will try to match it to a credit card or banking transaction. If it can't find a match, you can enter it manually. QBO stores all snapped receipts in the main system under *Menu, Transactions, Receipts*.

Track trip allows you to track your mileage every time you get in your car and then tell QBO whether it is business or personal. This may allow you to get some business deductions you may have missed or make it easier to prepare an expense account.

The rest of the items you will recognize from the computer version. You can enter invoices, income, and expense transactions. You can issue a sales receipt to a donor and have it emailed at a fundraising event.

Play around with the mobile app and see how it can work for you. Just remember to keep your password secure and follow all the necessary controls!

Next, we will talk about third party apps that integrate into QBO.

E. 3ᴿᴰ PARTY DEVELOPER APPS

Applications, referred to as apps, are created by Intuit or an approved third-party developer. They perform specific functions that are beyond the standard functionality of QBO. The greatest benefit of using apps is that they sync seamlessly with QBO. However, only apps that you authorize have the ability to access your QBO information. Intuit makes sure that apps follow industry best practices for accessing and storing data. You control the app's connection to QBO and can Go to *Menu, Apps, Find apps*.

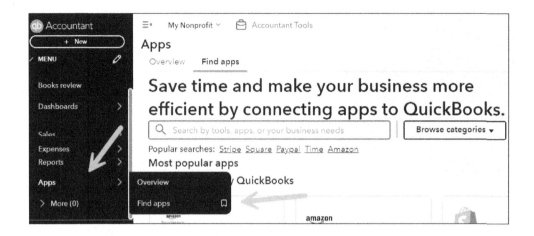

Take some time to search the options. If you type in Nonprofit, you will find apps specifically designed for donor management and receipts.

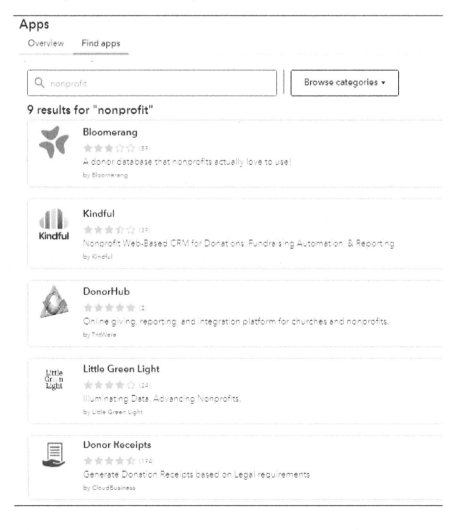

Each app has reviews. You can read overview information, watch a video demonstration, and review user feedback on each app. If one sounds promising, go to my FaceBook group, **Accountant Beside You QuickBooks Help** and see if any of the other bookkeepers are using it and can give you direction.

Some apps are free or have a basic option that is free. There is a monthly cost for others, but those usually have a 30-day free trial period. Also, you may find apps for services your organization already uses like PayPal or Square (both apps are free). Take time to explore, but I recommend you subscribe to a few apps that are truly beneficial and cost effective. Churches and organizations that use apps with QBO often find that the decrease in administrative hours outweighs the monthly cost.

I need to warn you. Credit card processers and other apps often upload the data into the system in a way that does not match the donors correctly (i.e., donor records have the donation posted net of the service fee instead of full donation). If that is the case, any time savings you may have gotten will be wasted trying to correct donor accounts.

Play around and utilize the free trials. It may be worth spending some money on an app like PayTraQer to give you more flexibility to book to classes and accounts in the way you want.

You did it!

Doesn't it feel great to realize you can set up QuickBooks for your nonprofit, enter transactions, run reports, prepare budgets, and all kinds of other useful tasks?

The system has much more functionality than I could possibly cover in this book, so experiment, explore, and have fun with it.

Index

Made in the USA
Coppell, TX
07 March 2024